dBase III Advanced Programming

Joseph-David Carrabis

Que Corporation
Indianapolis, Indiana

Library of Congress Catalog No.: 85-62364
ISBN 0-88022-169-0

89 88 87 86 85 8 7 6 5 4 3 2

Interpretation of the printing code: the rightmost double-digit number is the year of the book's printing; the rightmost single-digit number, the number of the book's printing. For example, a printing code of 84-3 shows that the third printing of the book occurred in 1984.

Dedication

To the man behind the curtain

Editorial Director
David F. Noble, Ph.D.

Editors
Jeannine Freudenberger, M.A.
Katherine Murray
Bill Nolan

Technical Editor
Ron Holmes

Screen reproductions in this book were created by means of the Printscreen program from DOMUS Software, Ltd., Ottawa, Ontario, Canada.

About the Author

Joseph-David Carrabis

Joseph-David Carrabis has been involved with computers for 15 years. His acquaintance with them began at Lincoln Labs, a government institute at Lexington, Mass. In 1980 he founded JDI, Inc., a business consulting and software design firm specializing in large-scale business systems. His clients, in locations ranging from New England to California and from Texas to Canada, have included several Fortune 500 companies.

Mr. Carrabis also has taught high school computer science and mathematics and has also done consultation for the Tuck School of Business, Dartmouth College. He has designed tutorials for Lotus 1-2-3, dBase II, and WordStar, and has written columns for Que Corporation's *IBM PC Update*.

A man of diverse interests, Mr. Carrabis has studied Old Testament theology and languages, applied mathematics and physics, and gravitational physics, as well as sign language. His first efforts in the computer field were directed toward making computers usable for the handicapped. He has enjoyed being a "designated hugger" for the Special Olympics. He holds a Black Belt in karate and is a member of the Computer Writers' Association and Science Fiction Writers of America.

Mr. Carrabis is now a product line director for Que Corporation.

Table of Contents

Foreword

My hope is that you will read this foreword before you buy the book. The information in this section will help you understand what this book covers better than will anything you can learn in a few minutes of standing in the bookstore, blocking the aisle, and scanning the book while you decide whether to purchase. I'm fully aware, though, that few people read a foreword unless it is written by a Stephen King or an Isaac Asimov. Well, this one is written by me, and so it is short.

I'm not writing a book chock-full of code for you to sit and copy. My purpose in writing this book is to help you write logical code in dBASE III.

How will I do this? First, I will define logical code. Then I will show the implications of writing logical code in the dBASE III environment. After that, I'll discuss how the dBASE III interpreter looks at code and show ways of minimizing execution time and memory consumption. Finally, I will demonstrate some little-known and seldom-used structures that can make dBASE III even more useful than most people think it is.

The book does contain many examples of code. You can use those examples if you wish. More important than the code, however, are the book's explanations and theory about the use of dBASE III. Wading through several pages of text to get to some useful code may seem boring to you. But the several pages of text explain how and why I chose that code and how and why it works. This knowledge is far more important for successful programming than is your mimicking me without knowing why I did what I did.

In the dBASE III code of Appendixes D through H, dBASE II programmers will see a stunning similarity with dBASE II code. I dCONVERTed good dBASE II code and edited it into good dBASE III code to prove my point about LIBrary files. Using many of the resources of dBASE II and III, I can maintain a "standard" library of files that are transportable between the two interpreters. Read the Introduction and Part I for more on why I do this.

If you haven't purchased dBASE III yet and are looking through books to see what dBASE III can and can't do, here are some words of advice:

1. dBASE III has a maximum of 128 fields per record. If you need more than 128 fields per record, rethink your application. Something is wrong.

2. dBASE III has a functional file-size limit of approximately five million bytes. The reference section of the user's manual says you have a two-billion-byte maximum on file size, but don't go wild with that information. If you regularly need a database management system capable of handling files larger than two million bytes, you should be prepared to *wait* for it to handle them. If you frequently need to sift through more than five million bytes at a whack, you need a computer bigger than a PC or clone, no matter what DBMS you're using.

3. Some users say dBASE III is slow. I discuss this fact in more detail later, but now I'll point out that most people do a few things expertly, many things well, most things acceptably, many things poorly, and a few things horribly. That goes for everybody. It also goes for DBMS software, dBASE III included. The joy of dBASE III is that it has a great deal of backing from various sectors, is from a company with a long and fruitful history, and is widely used and referenced. These facts are important when you're programming and you need help.

End of foreword. Good luck.

Acknowledgments

Many thanks to Jim, Jake, Chris, Natalie, John, Eric and Peter, of Chips; to Russ and Ben, of Data Spectrum, for letting me borrow books, equipment, and technical manuals during the writing of this book; and to Susan, who makes good coffee.

Trademark Acknowledgments

Que Corporation has made every effort to supply trademark information about company names, products, and services mentioned in this book. Trademarks indicated below were derived from various sources. Que Corporation cannot attest to the accuracy of this information.

dBASE III and dBASE II are trademarks of Ashton-Tate, Inc.
Printscreen is a trademark of DOMUS Software, Ltd., Ottawa, Ontario, Canada.
IBM is a trademark of International Business Machines Corporation.
1-2-3® is a registered trademark of Lotus Development Corporation.
WordStar is a trademark of MicroPro International, Inc.

Conventions Used in This Book

All declared variables are in uppercase letters.

All undeclared variables are in lowercase letters.

All dBASE III commands and functions are in uppercase.

All expressions and evaluations are in lowercase.

I have tried hard to be consistent, but I'm sure some things have slipped through. If something is unclear, make the logical choice. If that fails, experiment.

Introduction

First, did you read the foreword? Do so now if you haven't already.

What is advanced programming? When I started this project, my purpose had little to do with dBASE III. I was more concerned with the *advanced* part of the title. Advanced programming involves pseudocoding, data design, and system integration. Those and other twenty-six-dollar words are used primarily to impress others at parties. Knowing what the words mean won't help you get the job done, and not knowing exactly what they mean won't stop you from programming at an advanced level. You probably do those things anyway, either in your head or on paper, and knowing their names won't help you write better code.

My intent is neither to bore you nor to frighten you with words that have multiple meanings. I want you to learn to use all that this combination of language and machine—dBASE III and the IBM PC—has to offer. That knowledge is the sum total of advanced programming.

My purpose in this book is to give you some useful tools for generating better dBASE III code. What types of tools? I'll explain with a personal anecdote. I was incapable of learning math and physics by rote. It simply wasn't enough to watch someone do a grad or a curl or determine orthogonal equations. (BIG WORDS—don't be frightened!) I had to understand why and how those procedures worked before I could use them. That characteristic carries over into my method of programming. I'm not going to show you line after line of code without explaining, step by step, why I chose that code for a specific function. My intention is to get you to think in a specific way, or at least to be aware of some fundamental and powerful concepts.

Back to the first question. What is advanced programming? Experience has shown me that advanced programming has four parts:

1. Writing compact code
2. Writing to minimize execution time and maximize free disk space
3. Writing modular code (I use E. W. Dijkstra as my model)
4. Writing with a firm knowledge of the language

First, consider writing compact code. dBASE III lends itself to writing fat code in several ways; most obvious is the insertion of notes with the NOTE command or the *. Those of you who learned programming in a class were taught to incorporate rigorous documentation; get out of that habit.

However, dBASE III also lends itself to the writing of compact code. Chapters 1 and 2 of this book tell how. One trick for writing compact code has to do with the nature of dBASE III itself; it results in code that minimizes execution time and maximizes free disk space. Suppose you want to write time-efficient code and have ten active databases (ADBF, BDBF, CDBF, . . . JDBF). You are using JDBF and want to switch to ADBF. Which of the following two lines do you use? What is the actual difference in execution time?

```
SELECT ADBF
```

```
SELE A
```

For the answer, read the section called "Using the Four-Letter Word" in Chapter 1.

What does it mean to write modular code? For one thing, it's easier to debug and modify 12 lines than 200. Modular coding also speeds execution, especially if the function of the block of code (or module) isn't required every time dBASE executes the program.

For example, suppose you are given the task of developing a large accounting program for a company. You are told the different jobs the program must do. Controlling Accounts Receivable, Accounts

Payable, General Ledger, General Journal, Payroll, Inventory, Job Costing, and such are all separate jobs that together form the accounting program.

Obviously, you don't do Payroll every day; if your payroll is quite small, it may even be part of the Accounts Payable subsystem. You may do Accounts Receivable as payments come in, so you use this subsystem heavily one day and not at all the next two. You don't want to include all those jobs in your main program. Too many jobs slow execution and make the program unwieldy.

So how do you keep things as simple as possible when you start a project?

At the first meeting with your clients, you are given the skeleton of your program. The clients tell you what they want done. In other words, they give you a *menu* of what they need.

In this example, modular coding means that you first design a menu system for the various jobs. Each job becomes a module with its own menu system and tasks.

A menu system is the precursor, backbone, launching point—call it what you will—of a flowchart. Perhaps the most valuable thing you could have learned before opening this book is how to design flowcharts. In particular, I want you to design your charts on the basis of tasks. This book gives examples of task-oriented flowcharting. Also important is the distinction of tasks and jobs, which is covered later in this book.

To keep track of tasks and jobs and to construct a clean flowchart, you must write clear notes. This practice has to do with kicking the documentation habit. The accounting system is a good example: Your instinct is to document heavily so that others, looking at your code in the next millennium, can keep track of what you did and follow your program as it does what it does. The documentation further slows the running of the program.

Finally, to do advanced programming you must know your chosen language. What are the strengths and weaknesses of dBASE III?

First, consider the programming aspects of the language. dBASE III doesn't support the typical GOTO statement that is common in many other languages. Nor does dBASE III directly support JMPs or CALLs, as do assemblers. Don't write code that requires these commands. If you're accustomed to using them, learn to code linearly. Your GOTOs, JMPs, and CALLs must be replaced with the dBASE III command structures. This requirement leads us back to modular task-oriented flowcharts.

I have found dBASE III to be more linear in its logic flow than most languages. You can get from A to Z without ever touching B, C, and so on, and sample as many intermediaries as you wish. Those are things the language does nicely. But it dislikes spaghetti code. Don't expect dBASE III to go cheerfully from A to C to H to B to C to B to C to Z to D—you get the idea.

You can use dBASE III as a word processor because the program has a built-in text editor. I don't. You can use dBASE III as a spreadsheet program. I use other programs for spreadsheet functions. In a pinch, you can use dBASE III as a database management system. It's very good at that.

Many people describe dBASE III as an ADL, or applications development language, and it is that. Knowing that fact will not help you write better code, however.

Now comes a reverse maxim: The fact that dBASE III is an ADL is important to all that comes later in this book and is the key to the power of the language. dBASE III is a language specifically designed for manipulating data.

dBASE III is not meant to tweak the brain of the machine or to juggle ports, although the language does have those useful capabilities. The program is not meant to be a number cruncher, although its arithmetic capabilities are extensive. dBASE III is not a general-purpose language, a jack-of-all-trades. dBASE III is a master of one trade: database management. I hope this book will help you use dBASE III as such. That concept again brings us back to forethought and the creation of good task-oriented flowcharts before writing code.

At various points in this book, I use programs in languages other than dBASE III. In truth, most of the other programs I create are written in a variety of dialects and subtongues. Because I can't assume you have available a variety of languages and compilers, all ancillary programs in this book are in IBM BASIC, with one exception. The CRYPTOR.ASM listing in Appendix A is given just because I like assemblers, I don't like to document, and I acknowledge the power of assembly language to do things other languages can't. The object code generated by the IBM BASIC compiler gives programmers familiar with MASM a launching point for their own explorations. All other programs are in IBM BASIC. If you are reading a book on dBASE III, you must have IBM BASIC available. The BASIC code shows you the flow of the program. You can choose another language and write code from there.

I

Advanced Programming Techniques

In Part I, we examine in more depth the four principles of advanced programming presented in the Introduction. You may already be familiar with many of the topics covered. Others may be hazy in your mind. In this part, we lay the foundations for most dBASE III programming techniques. These foundations are used in the turnkey systems that are explained in Part II.

The first consideration is writing compact code. That is not something we programmers do instinctively. Our programs tend to resemble Charles Dickens' novels—they're too long. We should write more like Hemingway; don't put in fifty words what you can say in two.

Writing compact code consists of three things: defining the problem, recognizing the solution, and coding for that solution. We only code for the problem at hand, and we don't concern ourselves with multitudes of possibilities.

Then we have to consider how our solution interacts with the language and the machine. Careful thought leads to solutions that are simple and that make efficient use of the machine. Here again we can use Hemingway as a model (or Philip Glass, if you're musically inclined). We must think as minimalists.

We have to learn how dBASE III works in order to learn how to make it work at its best. Getting the most out of dBASE III has two equal parts:

1. *Code only for the job at hand.* Don't concern yourself with I/O, screen or printer graphics and output, or anything else, if your purpose is to alter data. All other operations can be coded in other modules or subroutines. Accomplishing this entails not only writing modular code but also knowing when and how dBASE III looks at subroutines, procedures, and their kin.

2. *Write with a firm knowledge of dBASE III.* I assume you either are comfortable with dBASE III or are a quick study. If not, some parts of this book may seem opaque to you, especially the sections dealing with dBASE III's strengths. Those sections deal with using dBASE III's undocumented abilities. Some of these abilities include advanced database operations, operations on many active databases (such as linking, cross referencing, and data chaining), and descriptions and analysis of looping functions.

1
Writing Compact Code

Source documentation—the explanations included in working code—is one of the great banes of writing compact programs. Unfortunately, we cannot guarantee our immortality; we must therefore document our programs, both in our source code and externally, so that others can easily modify our code if necessary.

Methods of Documentation

One way to solve the problem is to separate our code and documentation. We can then place the documentation at the end of our code after a RETURN, QUIT, or CANCEL.

This method, however, is usually more trouble than it's worth for the programmer and more confusing than helpful for the reader. Explanations of our logic given after the fact need to be more carefully worded. That usually means saying in three different ways what really needs to be said only once. ("I know you think you heard what I said, but what you thought you heard is not what I meant to say.")

Also consider the poor readers. They must determine which DO WHILE N2<100 of the 20 listed in the program is the one you're referring to. And if your documentation is inaccurate, the readers are even worse off.

Fortunately, most programmers place explanations where they're needed. Even if we don't document internally, we use the * simply to isolate code segments. Consider the following program.

```
***BLOCKER1.PRG
***WRITTEN BY JOSEPH-DAVID CARRABIS
***HANOVER, NH 03755
**
***SET UP
**
SET TALK OFF
STORE 0 TO N0,N1,N2
INPUT "What is our starting value -> " TO NUM
NUM2=NUM*NUM
**
***BLOCK 0
**
DO WHILE NUM>1
   ? "BLOCK0"+STR(N0,4,0)
   N0=N0+1
**
***BLOCK 1
**
   DO WHILE NUM<NUM2
      ? "BLOCK1"+STR(N1,4,0)
      NUM=2*NUM
      N1=N1+1
   ENDDO 1
**
***BLOCK 2
**
   IF NUM2<(2*NUM)
      ? "BLOCK2"+STR(N2,4,0)
      NUM=NUM2/NUM
      N2=N2+1
   ENDIF 2
**
ENDDO 0
**
SET TALK ON
```

This program, which juggles the variables NUM and NUM2, demonstrates a fairly typical method of documenting source code. Debugging the program is fairly easy because we always know where the program is, and we can determine where it trashes out by providing a listing of where the program has been, as in figure 1.1.

```
->do blocker

What is our starting value -> 10000

BLOCK0          0
BLOCK1          0
BLOCK1          1
BLOCK1          2
BLOCK1          3
BLOCK1          4
BLOCK1          5
BLOCK1          6
BLOCK1          7
BLOCK1          8
BLOCK1          9
BLOCK1          10
BLOCK1          11
BLOCK1          12
BLOCK1          13
BLOCK2          0

->


->
```

Fig. 1.1. Output of BLOCKER1.PRG, showing a simple trace for debugging.

After we've debugged our code and know it does the job, we can consider making the code compact. Stripping the notes from the code reduces the program from 36 to 19 lines, a savings of about 50 percent. Next, we pull out our debugging lines. That deletion gets us down to 12 lines, the 12 lines that actually do what we want.

The following IBM BASIC program, STRIPPER.BAS, strips out excess lines. The lines I use to debug code are always the same. STRIPPER can be expanded as necessary and is a useful tool that you would be wise to modify for your own purposes.

```
1 REM        STRIPPER.BAS
10 OPEN "BLOCKER1.PRG" FOR INPUT AS 1
20 OPEN "NEW-01.DB3" FOR OUTPUT AS 2
30 REM  INSERT ADDITIONAL CODE HERE, IF NEEDED
40 N$="***"
50 B$="? 'BLOCK"
60 Z$="N0"
70 O$="N1"
80 T$="N2"
90 WHILE NOT EOF(1)
100 LINE INPUT#1,L$
110 IF (INSTR(L$,N$)=0)AND(INSTR(L$,B$)=0)AND(INSTR(L$,Z$)=0)AND
(INSTR(L$,O$)=0)AND(INSTR(L$,T$)=0) GOTO 130
120 GOTO 90
130 PRINT#2,L$
140 LPRINT L$
150 WEND
160 END
```

STRIPPER.BAS works as follows. My debugging and noting follow certain patterns; hence the variables defined in lines 40 through 80. Extra variables can be easily inserted in the BASIC program if a particular application forces me to alter my method. Lines 90 to 150 form a loop that remains active until the program reaches the end of my dBASE source-code file. The code of that loop translates as follows: If none of my debugging or note-taking methods is used in a line (110), print that line to a file (130) and to the printer (140); otherwise, get the next line of code (120). Lines 10 through 30 can be changed to adapt STRIPPER.BAS for multiple input, to redirect source and target drives, and so on. I print the stripped program (140) to check the integrity of the source code.

A similar program is dFaster.dBetter, which is available from Micro db Systems (Midland, Michigan). dFaster.dBetter also decreases execution time and file size by removing comments. The purpose of dFaster.dBetter is not simply to strip notes from program listings, however. In addition, it compacts code and demonstrates ways to increase dBASE programming efficiency. It does more than STRIPPER does because dFaster.dBetter was not intended to serve the same function as STRIPPER. dFaster.dBetter was used to produce the listings in Appendixes C through G.

dBASE III gives you one other method of documentation. With some, but not all, dBASE III commands, you can include notes beside the command on the same line. This method takes the form

```
COMMAND * explanation
```

COMMAND is a dBASE III command or function, and the * tells dBASE that the rest of the line can be ignored. dBASE III has a habit of reading only what the program needs to get a job done. However, this method doesn't work with commands that do comparisons or evaluations. For instance, you cannot use the command

```
CASE NEWKEY=254 *F2 PRESSED
```

because dBASE III "assumes" you are checking to see whether NEWKEY is equal to the string 254^I*F2 PRESSED. This method of documentation also uses up more space on the disk, because dBASE III is interpreted, not compiled. The program doesn't use your notes, but it acknowledges their presence when writing and reading files.

By this point, you may be tiring of my harangue on compact code. Why do I repeatedly stress this? Compact code is space- and time-efficient. Space is a priority both on disk and in memory. Time is a priority to anyone who pays by the hour to have information put into a database and manipulated. Neither dBASE III nor the PC needs or likes copious notes.

Timesavings

Before describing eye-popping timesavings, I should explain that my average system project contains from 10,000 to 30,000 lines of code. These are obviously large-scale projects that chew up most of the computer's time and space. Because my system programs are so long, I go out of my way to decrease execution time.

Experience has shown me that the extra effort is worthwhile. Clients and peers have commented on a noticeable decrease in execution time. To have your fireworks appreciated is always nice.

Most programmers—myself included—document their programs externally and internally. So, the first technique worth knowing is as follows. After you have the program totally debugged and everyone is happy with the way it works, make a backup copy. Then take out all the comment lines from the working copy.

Consider program BLOCKER1.PRG. If you key in the program, SET STEP ON, and DO BLOCKER1.PRG, you can see that the PC actually "looks at" each comment line. The PC doesn't do anything with the comment lines, but looking at them slows down the operation.

Now look at BLOCKER2.PRG. It was generated by STRIPPER.BAS, using BLOCKER1.PRG as a source file.

```
SET TALK OFF
INPUT "What is our starting value -> " TO NUM
NUM2=NUM*NUM
DO WHILE NUM>1
   DO WHILE NUM<NUM2
      NUM=2*NUM
   ENDDO 1
   IF NUM2<(2*NUM)
      NUM=NUM2/NUM
   ENDIF 2
ENDDO Ø
SET TALK ON
```

What is the actual savings in time? The following simple time-checking program, TIMETEST.PRG, determines average run time. Changes made to both BLOCKER1.PRG and BLOCKER2.PRG are minor and—I hope—obvious.

```
SET TALK OFF
INPUT "How many runs shall we make? -> " TO Q
STORE Ø TO TFSS, TFMM
STORE 1 TO NQ
**
DO WHILE NQ<Q+1
   STORE 1 TO N
**
   STORE TIME( ) TO TØ
***BLOCKER. PRG
**
***SETUP
**
SET TALK OFF
STORE Ø TO NØ, N1, N2
NUM=NQ
NUM2=NUM*NUM
**
***BLOCK Ø
**
```

```
DO WHILE NUM>1
   ? "BLOCKØ"+STR(NØ,4,Ø)
   NØ=NØ+1
**
***BLOCK 1
**
   DO WHILE NUM<NUM2
      ? "BLOCK1"+STR(N1,4,Ø)
      NUM=2*NUM
      N1=N1+1
   ENDDO 1
**
***BLOCK 2
**
   IF NUM2<(2*NUM)
      ? "BLOCK2"+STR(N2,4,Ø)
      NUM=NUM2/NUM
      N2=N2+1
   ENDIF 2
**
ENDDO Ø
**
SET TALK ON
   STORE TIME( ) TO T1
**
   STORE VAL(SUBSTR(TØ,7,2)) TO TØSS
   STORE VAL(SUBSTR(T1,7,2)) TO T1SS
   STORE VAL(SUBSTR(TØ,4,2)) TO TØMM
   STORE VAL(SUBSTR(T1,4,2)) TO T1MM
**
   IF T1SS<TØSS
      T1SS=T1SS+6Ø
      T1MM=T1MM-1
   ENDIF
**
   TFMM=TFMM+T1MM-TØMM
   TFSS=TFSS+T1SS-TØSS
   NQ=NQ+1
ENDDO
**
TFSS=TFSS/Q
MINUTES=Ø
**
```

```
DO WHILE TFSS>59
   TFSS=TFSS-60
   MINUTES=MINUTES+1
ENDDO
**
TFMM=(TFMM/Q)+MINUTES
CLEAR
@ 10,0 SAY "AVERAGE TIME ->                                        SS"
@ 10,20 SAY TFSS
```

TIMETEST.PRG gives an average run time of 1.35 seconds for BLOCKER1.PRG on 100 runs. The same program, running BLOCKER2.PRG, gives an average run time of 0.54 seconds, a 250 percent gain in execution speed. Incidentally, the figure for space savings is 295 percent. The documented file is 640 bytes long; the stripped file is 217 bytes.

Using the Four-Letter Word

dBASE III supports the use of shortened commands: SELE for SELECT, INPU for INPUT, STOR for STORE. What happens if we strip all our commands to the first four characters when we code? Consider the following example. In the Introduction you were asked which of the two commands the computer can read faster:

```
SELECT ADBF
SELE A
```

Obviously, humans scan the second line quicker than the first. Is this fact also true for the computer? The average execution times are .01030 seconds for the first line and .00730 seconds for the second. Granted, both times are minuscule—to us. To the PC with a 4.77 MHz clock, however, the times represent, respectively, 49,131 and 34,821 cycles. The difference is a great deal of time to a PC.

Eliminating Dead Space in a Program File

Clipping my code did not alone buy all my kudos for writing fast programs.

The programs in this book, as you'll see, indent blocks of code. I write something like the following:

```
DO CASE
   CASE condition 1
      condition 1 instructions
   CASE condition 2
      condition 2 instructions
   .
   .
   .
ENDCASE
```

Another format is

```
DO WHILE condition
   instructions
ENDDO
```

and so on.

I write code that way only for other users—for magazine articles and the classes I teach. My own choice is not to indent; in my own programs, I use ** to separate blocks of code.

People tell me, "You must learn to indent properly to make your programs more readable."

"By whom," I ask, "you or the computer?"

Does dBASE III care about indenting? Yes.

Indenting is good if a human is going to try to execute your programs line by line and wants to follow what is going on. But dBASE has a different problem with indented lines. Given the line

```
         @ 22,20 GET meadrink
```

dBASE dutifully looks at each of the nine preceding spaces before doing what is asked. Even though you don't see anything before @ 22,20, the PC senses nine 20Hs (the hexadecimal value of a blank space). This dead space is detrimental both on disk and during execution. Total the dead space in all your programs and the amount can be staggering. The moral? Don't indent.

2
How To Code Efficiently

What does it mean to code efficiently?

What does it mean to do anything "efficiently?"

Let's take the latter first. Given the choice of lifting a loaded sea trunk in a deadlift or using a come-along, I'd choose the come-along. It enables me to do less work and achieve the same result: lifting the sea trunk. Given the choice of a come-along or a three-block pulley, I would take the pulley—again, because I have to do even less work to raise the sea trunk.

I'm making more efficient use of my strength by using the best tools to get the work done. This is the key to efficiency in anything: using minimum effort to achieve maximum results with minimum waste.

Now to the former question. In programming, any problem has various solutions, any one of which will do the job. But you don't want to write 20K of code when 5K will do the same job. Part of efficiency is learning to notice patterns. Most applications have many similarities. There is usually no need to write new code when something you have written before will do the job.

This chapter will deal primarily with flowchart design and how to make better use of the dBASE programming environment. Primary to this discussion are the concepts of "task" and "job." Tasks (and their structure) are the code that does the work. Jobs are the work to be done by the task.

You want to make coffee, for example. The tasks include measuring and grinding coffee beans; rinsing the pot and setting the filter; getting cold, clear water and heating it to 190F; pouring a cupful of water over the grounds to set them in the filter; and so on (yes, I'm a coffee-aholic, but at least I do it right!). The job is making coffee.

Another part of coding efficiently is recognizing the limits of your environment. Does the PC or dBASE III limit your solutions?

All of these things are nice to know before you start a project. If you've spent much time programming for others, you've learned that clients usually do not comprehend how long the job will take or exactly what they want. You tell them "two months" and they hear "yesterday." As a programmer, you should also be aware that customers are probably going to want more than they anticipated or want what they asked for to be done differently.

Your clients give you a list of things they want done. They aren't concerned with how the program does the job, but they do want the program to be easy to use and to generate output they can easily understand.

The clients give you the following list of jobs:

1. Generate a customer mailing list
2. Report total sales by factory
3. Report total sales by customer
4. List all factories
5. Generate sales commissions
6. Generate unpaid commissions
7. List all active customers
8. List all inactive customers
9. Keep an updatable customer database
10. Keep an updatable factory database
11. Keep an updatable item sold database

12. Keep an updatable sales force database
13. Provide selective backup ability
14. Provide selective retrieval from backup

The problem, then, is to translate the client's wish list into a working program. dBASE III offers several possible solutions. But does it provide a clue as to which solution is better than the others? Yes, it does. Some clues are in the similarities between the things the client wants done. It would appear that the tasks are repetitive, even if the jobs aren't.

As an experiment, let's look at the Bigger Hammer method of programming. A straightforward approach to the whole problem is to create the following code using the DO CASE . . . (OTHERWISE) . . . ENDCASE command.

```
DO CASE
   CASE CHOICE=1
      DO MAILLIST
**
   CASE CHOICE=2
      DO FACTSALE
**
   CASE CHOICE=3
      DO CUSTSALE
**
   CASE CHOICE=4
      DO FACTLIST
**
   CASE CHOICE=5
      DO COMM
**
   CASE CHOICE=6
      DO UNPDCOMM
**
   CASE CHOICE=7
      DO ACCUST
**
   CASE CHOICE=8
      DO INACCUST
**
   CASE CHOICE=9
      DO CUSTOMER
```

```
**
   CASE CHOICE=10
      DO FACTORY
**
   CASE CHOICE=11
      DO ITEMSOLD
**
   CASE CHOICE=12
      DO SALESFRCE
**
   CASE CHOICE=13
      DO BACKUP
**
   CASE CHOICE=14
      DO RETRIEVE
**
   OTHERWISE
      ERROR MESSAGE
ENDCASE
```

The Flowchart

The preceding code sequence is workable but heavy and unnecessary. The code demonstrates thinking in jobs rather than individual tasks. The distinction between job and task is vital; a flowchart and examples will make it clear. If we look at what the company has asked for, we can create a task-oriented flowchart. We also know that dBASE III is a database manipulator, and we keep that fact in mind as we create the flowchart shown in figure 2.1.

Ideas should start popping into your head as soon as you have written the flowchart. (And remember, you haven't even started to code yet!) What ideas? For example, you have a MAILLIST MODULE. Would your client like to be able to send mailings to factories or salespeople, as well as customers? You have a LISTING MODULE. Perhaps a listing of items sold, broken down by volume and price, might be useful to your client. Even more options can spin directly off the tasks (MAIL LIST, SALES, COMMISSIONS, etc.) listed in the flowchart.

Jobs and Tasks

I hope you are beginning to see why I differentiate between jobs and tasks. A task is necessary to get a job done. Digging a hole is a task. The job may be planting a tree, digging a well, or putting in a swimming pool. Each job requires that you dig a hole.

Look at the flowchart. Do you see that the 14 jobs listed in the flowchart are repetitive? Those 14 jobs can be performed by 7 tasks. We can also place the retrieval and backup jobs in 1 task, bringing us down to 6 tasks to handle 14 jobs. (We all have our own little idiosyncrasies. One of mine is packing many jobs into a few lines of code.)

By thinking and coding in tasks, you make modifications easier. Working in tasks also saves you time on future projects because you build up a library of tasks common to all environments. For instance, every customer wants easy ways to add, delete, edit, and scan records. One block of code for each can be used for several different databases. For this reason, many of my projects use the same DATABASE ACCESS MODULE (see Appendix C).

Whether you flowchart in your head or on paper doesn't matter. The purpose of a flowchart is to provide a skeleton to be fleshed out as you go along.

The Code

Remember also that your primary objective is to get a job done. Your code shouldn't be filled with redundancies and superfluous lines, but code does not have to be exact the first time through. Good programmers know that the product they deliver is not always the best it could be. But the program does what was intended, and that capability is the bottom line.

At this point I introduce you to the first of JDI's Standard Rules of Programming, Number 100:

> If it works, don't fix it.

Don't worry about perfection.

Remember to think in tasks, and your code will be better. This thought brings us back to the development stage. Our flowchart is good and clean. Now we begin actual coding.

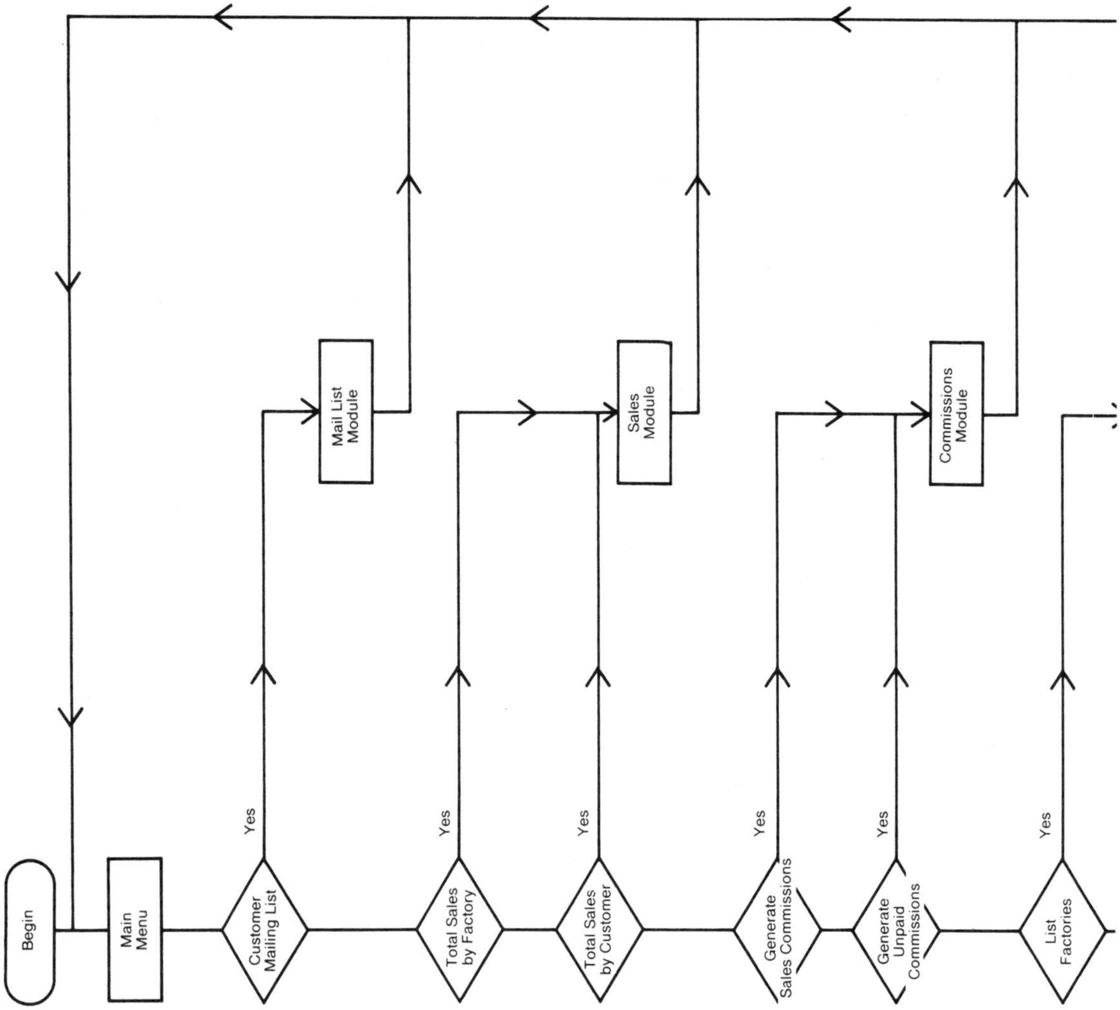
Begin
Main Menu
Customer Mailing List
Yes
Mail List Module
Total Sales by Factory
Yes
Total Sales by Customer
Yes
Sales Module
Generate Sales Commissions
Yes
Generate Unpaid Commissions
Yes
Commissions Module
List Factories
Yes

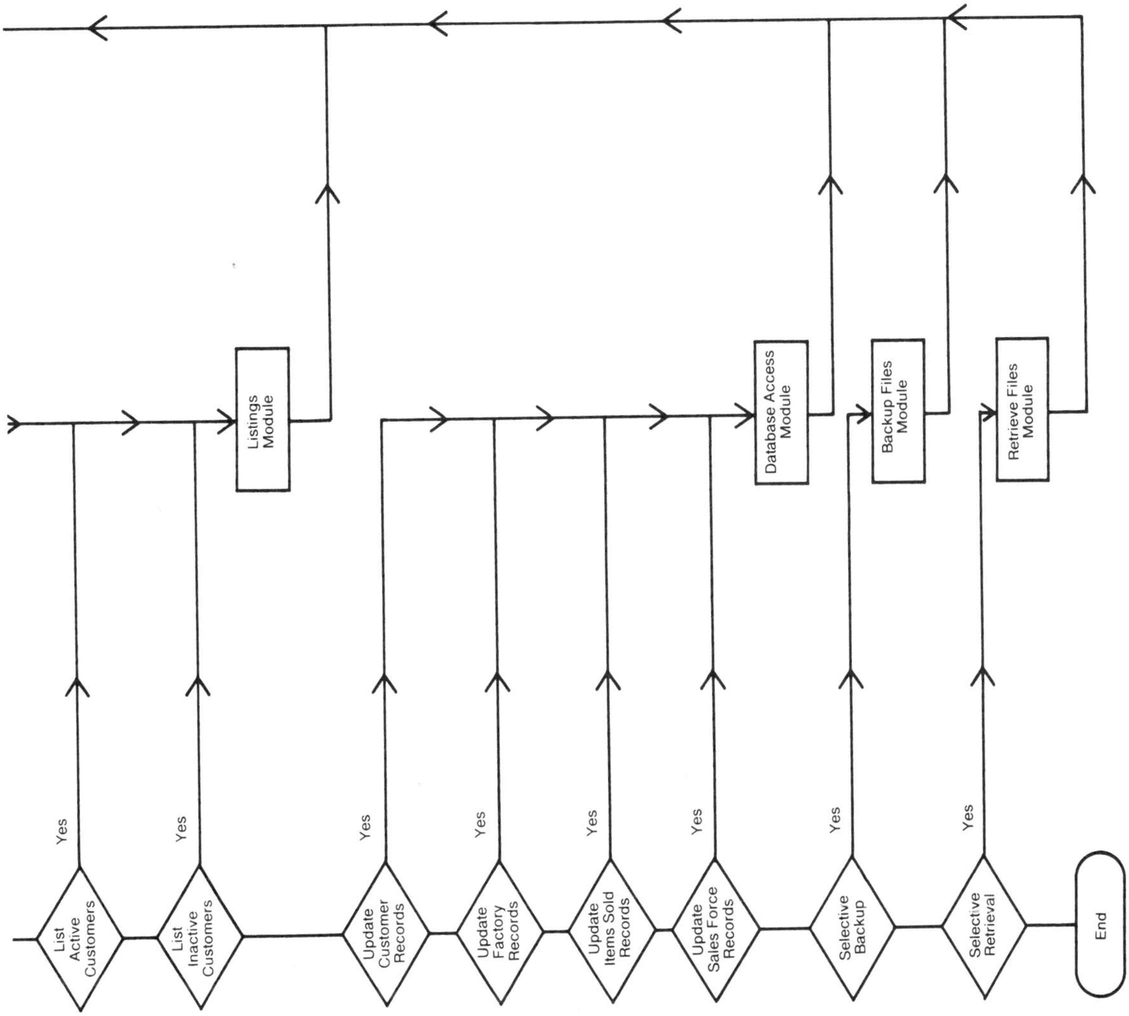

Fig. 2.1. A task-oriented flowchart.

The User Interface

Looking at the flowchart again, notice that it performs two functions: it provides a user interface and it calls subroutines. Creating the user interface is easy enough:

```
CLEAR
TEXT
========================================================================
||     N O R T H E A S T   S A L E S   M A I N   M E N U            ||
========================================================================
||                                                                  ||
||                                                                  ||
||            Ø. Exit                                               ||
||            1. Customer Mailing List                              ||
||            2. Factory Totals by Month and Year                   ||
||            3. Customer Totals by Month and Year                  ||
||            4. Commission Report                                  ||
||            5. Unpaid Commission Report                           ||
||            6. Factory Listing                                    ||
||            7. Active Customer Listing                            ||
||            8. Inactive Customer Listing                          ||
||            9. Update Customers                                   ||
||           1Ø. Update Factories                                   ||
||           11. Update Items Sold                                  ||
||           12. Update Salespeople                                 ||
||           13. Back Up All Files                                  ||
||           14. Retrieve All Files                                 ||
||                                                                  ||
========================================================================
ENDTEXT
```

The first thing to notice is that I've rearranged the list. Now similar tasks are next to each other on the menu. This arrangement is helpful when I begin writing the code to call the different subroutines.

To create the menu, why do I choose TEXT. . .ENDTEXT rather than a rack of @ SAYs? The logic of my choice has two points. Most obvious is that I'm not getting any information from the user; all I'm doing is printing the screen. The powers of an @ SAY statement are the GET and the statement's usefulness in a format file, in a FRAMER file (see Appendix H), and in printing.

The other reason not to use @ SAY has to do with what I call input aesthetics. You can more easily enter the contents of the screen exactly as you want it to appear by using TEXT . . . ENDTEXT rather than @ SAYs. In this case, however, I also break one of my own rules. The @ SAY command executes far faster than the TEXT. . . ENDTEXT. Once I am satisfied that my TEXT . . . ENDTEXT works well and produces the screen I want, I usually run the text through dBASE III's SED (the Screen EDitor included in the dBASE III package) or a similar utility. Such utilities allow the programmer to print a screen and then transform it into a rack of @ SAYs. (See APPENDIX K for a discussion of the SED utility.)

Subroutines

On to the second function shown in the flowchart, which is equally easy to code. We're going to call subroutines that perform each task. dBASE III offers two methods of enabling the user to select one of several options: DO CASE . . . (OTHERWISE) . . . ENDCASE and IF . . . (ELSE) . . . ENDIF.

The following code segments illustrate three ways these options may be used.

1. DO CASE . . . (OTHERWISE) . . . ENDCASE

```
DO CASE

   CASE CHOICE=0
      RETURN
**
   CASE CHOICE=1
      DO MAILLIST
**
   CASE CHOICE<4
      DO TOTALS
**
   CASE CHOICE<6
      DO COMMRPRT
**
   CASE CHOICE<9
      DO LISTINGS
**
   CASE CHOICE<13
      DO MAIN
```

```
**
   CASE CHOICE=13
      DO BACKUP
**
   CASE CHOICE=14
      DO RETRIEVE
**
   OTHERWISE
      ERROR MESSAGE
ENDCASE
```

2. IF . . . (ELSE) . . . ENDIF #1

```
IF CHOICE=Ø
   RETURN
ELSE
**
   IF CHOICE=1
      DO MAILLIST
      LOOP
   ELSE
**
      IF CHOICE<4
         DO TOTALS
         LOOP
      ELSE
**
         IF CHOICE<6
            DO COMMRPRT
            LOOP
         ELSE
**
            IF CHOICE<9
               DO LISTINGS
               LOOP
            ELSE
**
               IF CHOICE<13
                  DO MAIN
                  LOOP
               ELSE
```

```
**
                    IF CHOICE=13
                       DO BACKUP
                       LOOP
                    ELSE
**
                       IF CHOICE=14
                          DO RETRIEVE
                       ELSE
                          uERROR MESSAGE
                       ENDIF14
**
                    ENDIF13
**
                 ENDIF<13
**
              ENDIF<9
**
           ENDIF<6
**
        ENDIF<4
**
   ENDIF1
**
ENDIFØ
```

A better alternative to the preceding code is to use the IF . . . (ELSE) . . . ENDIF structure as follows:

3. IF . . . (ELSE) . . . ENDIF #2

```
IF CHOICE=Ø
   RETURN
ENDIF
**
IF CHOICE=1
   DO MAILLIST
   LOOP
ENDIF
**
IF CHOICE<4
   DO TOTALS
   LOOP
ENDIF
```

```
**
IF CHOICE<6
   DO COMMRPRT
   LOOP
ENDIF
**
IF CHOICE<9
   DO LISTINGS
   LOOP
ENDIF
**
IF CHOICE<13
   DO MAIN
   LOOP
ENDIF
**
IF CHOICE=13
   DO BACKUP
   LOOP
ENDIF
**
IF CHOICE=14
   DO RETRIEVE
   LOOP
ENDIF
**
ERROR MESSAGE
```

Counting the lines of the code segments, we note that the DO CASE . . . (OTHERWISE) . . . ENDCASE has 20 lines. IF . . . (ELSE) . . . ENDIF #2 has 32 lines, and IF . . . (ELSE) . . . ENDIF #1 has 39 lines. The obvious choice, therefore, is the DO CASE . . . (OTHERWISE) . . . ENDCASE.

The fact that we code in tasks facilitates the use of CASEs. When dBASE III encounters CASEs, the program finds the first CASE that meets the condition, executes the commands of that CASE, and exits from the DO CASE . . . (OTHERWISE) . . . ENDCASE command. Once a CASE has been selected, all other CASEs are ignored. This method is an efficient means for assigning different tasks.

Because we place the most frequently used jobs on the top of the pile, much of the code is ignored. That same method is used with the IF . . . (ELSE) . . . ENDIF command when we introduce LOOP.

dBASE stops any further looking and brings us back to the top of the flowchart. For those who question my using LOOP, remember that we're developing a front end to a much larger system.

Linking the Functions

We've spoken of the two necessary functions of our flowchart: creating a user interface and calling subroutines. We haven't talked about how these two functions are linked. We link them with a DO WHILE . . . ENDDO command.

If we follow the steps outlined thus far, the finished product is as follows:

```
DO WHILE .T.

   CHOICE=0
   CLEAR
   TEXT

======================================================================
||     N O R T H E A S T    S A L E S    M A I N    M E N U      ||
======================================================================
||                                                                ||
||                                                                ||
||           0. Exit                                              ||
||           1. Customer Mailing List                             ||
||           2. Factory Totals by Month and Year                  ||
||           3. Customer Totals by Month and Year                 ||
||           4. Commission Report                                 ||
||           5. Unpaid Commission Report                          ||
||           6. Factory Listing                                   ||
||           7. Active Customer Listing                           ||
||           8. Inactive Customer Listing                         ||
||           9. Update Customers                                  ||
||          10. Update Factories                                  ||
||          11. Update Items Sold                                 ||
||          12. Update Salespeople                                ||
||          13. Back Up All Files                                 ||
||          14. Retrieve All Files                                ||
||                                                                ||
=======================Your Choice -> == <-=======================
```

```
   ENDTEXT
   @ 22,44 GET CHOICE PICTURE "##"
   READ
**
   DO CASE
      CASE CHOICE=0
         RETURN
**
      CASE CHOICE=1
         DO MAILLIST
**
      CASE CHOICE<4
         DO TOTALS
**
      CASE CHOICE<6
         DO COMMRPRT
**
      CASE CHOICE<9
         DO LISTINGS
**
      CASE CHOICE<13
         DO MAIN
**
      CASE CHOICE=13
         DO BACKUP
**
      CASE CHOICE=14
         DO RETRIEVE
**
      OTHERWISE
         WAIT "Valid Choices are 0-14. Press any key to continue."
   ENDCASE
**
ENDDO
```

I've omitted the code with which you select specific databases for each job. That code is the same no matter what method you choose, unless you make each subroutine access separately the necessary data and related files.

You may also have noticed that I can't count lines of code. No, actually, I just don't count lines that are preceded by the *. Those lines come out after the program is debugged and running smoothly, anyway. It is important to remember that all source documentation, even if it's only some asterisks separating blocks of code, will be removed once the program is working as the client intends.

Last, a minor point. I initialize CHOICE to the value needed to exit from the program—one more bailout for those too fearful to press anything but Return.

I have emphasized a modular, task-oriented approach to programming. My intent is to get you thinking in small, easily coded sections, instead of seeing a whole job before you and growing faint.

One last word on modular programming. I have said that I tend to pack as much as I can into as little code as possible. That is one side of the scale, and the scale has to balance. The other side is to keep your code and logic as simple as possible. Don't follow the old BASIC logic of

```
FOR I=1 TO 10: STEP1: STEP2: STEP3: ... : STEP99:NEXT
```

Debugging that can be nauseating.

Input/Output, dBASE III, and the PC

We need to bear in mind two things regarding input/output and the PC. One thing has to do with the particular input/output methods of the PC; the other concerns sequential and random access of disks.

dBASE III is a disk-intensive language designed to run on a computer with a minimum of 256K of memory. The original dBASE was designed to run on a 64K machine. The only way to accomplish this feat was to have dBASE go to the disk for code and data because there was no room for them in the machine's memory.

dBASE III retains that method. A minimum of 256K of memory is necessary just so there'll be room for all the background tasks needed to make the program run. Once those tasks are in memory, dBASE III reads in as much of your code as the computer has room for. The obvious moral is to get a PC with 512K or so of memory.

Unfortunately, dBASE III doesn't treat data the same way. Data remains on the disk and is accessed as needed. One way around this limitation is to change the CONFIG.SYS file. Another way is to buy or write RAM-disk or V-disk software.

Changing the CONFIG.SYS File to Manage I/O

Changing the CONFIG.SYS file does not physically alter the way dBASE III gets data from a disk. What changes is the number of times dBASE III has to look for data on the disk. This change has to do with buffers and the way the PC uses them.

Another reason for considering modification of the CONFIG.SYS file has to do with programming in tasks. I ask you to code in tasks; however, if you open enough files and ask dBASE III to perform enough tasks, you run into a wall because the number of files you can open at one time is limited.

Handling Files and Buffers

You can increase the number of files and buffers open at one time by altering the CONFIG.SYS file. (dBASE II programmers, who are accustomed to SELECTing either PRIMARY or SECONDARY, often have some difficulty in getting used to dBASE III's ability to manage ten active databases.) With 256K of memory, you have no real reason to alter the CONFIG.SYS file; altering your programs to open fewer files is a better choice. However, when more memory is available, you can rewrite the CONFIG.SYS file as follows:

```
FILES=20
BUFFERS=24
```

(Include whatever lines were previously in the file.)

The problem with limited memory and many active files and buffers is that both files and buffers take up room in memory whether they are used or not. This limitation pertains to more than just dBASE III files. Every time a file, any file, is opened, dBASE III loses some room in the memory of the machine.

For example, the line

```
FILES=20
```

tells DOS to allow twenty open files; DOS passes the message along to dBASE. Those twenty files get eaten quickly, however. You start with DOS. There goes one file. Next is DBASE.EXE. Two down. You'd like to know what you're doing, so you have DBASE.OVL working. Three down. Need some help? Add HELP.DBS and four away. This scenario is simple, but you get the picture. Add a few databases; their index files; a dBASE program file or two, each of which calls in a subroutine; a format file; perhaps a memo file; maybe old files from which you're creating a new database; and so on. Available files get chewed up pretty fast.

Programs that open too many files without any place to put them, because of limited memory or an incorrect CONFIG.SYS file, result in the message

```
TOO MANY FILES OPEN
```

Far more aggravating is getting no message or warning whatsoever and seeing dBASE slow to a crawl because of an overtaxed memory.

With a low-memory system, you'd rather have buffers open than files. With buffers the PC (and therefore dBASE III) can keep track of the information around the last-requested information. Sound cryptic? This concept has to do with contiguous INDEXed files and is discussed in more detail later in this book (see "Operations with Index Files").

A nice way to think of files and buffers is to think of files as Indian clubs and buffers as drinking glasses. The PC juggles Indian clubs and drinks out of glasses. When your CONFIG.SYS file supports only ten open files and you throw in an eleventh Indian club, everything falls to the ground. When you have only ten glasses in front of you and you want to taste an eleventh drink, you have to empty a glass before you can refill it.

A somewhat more worthy explanation is that the PC keeps track of information internally as much as possible. This aspect of the PC's design makes things happen faster because the machine doesn't have to read and write to the disk as often. Of course, a good chunk of the computer's memory is used for housekeeping. When you are opening and closing data files, command files, text files, and format files, you are using up memory to keep track of where things are on the disks. The maximum number of files you can have active with dBASE III is 20. This number is cut in half when you use just database files. But it's a bear to have all those files open as well as subsequent readings and writings to disk for each file.

The problem is one of knowing and working within the PC's limits. You want to design your system so that memory is utilized as much as possible. Each disk access slows down the program; but when much of the memory is used for housekeeping, you run the risk on a 256K machine of forcing DOS to throw the interpreter, HELP, and other necessary files back out to the disk. The trade-off is between memory management and program execution speed. This is a delicate problem that you can often avoid when you know something about DOS.

The problem is remedied by using buffers. But buffers exist only in the memory of the machine, never on the disk. Buffers make the PC work faster, but they chew up memory. The moral? Decrease the number of buffers if you need more files open. The less RAM you have, the smaller the buffers must be and the slower the machine will run. As a result, 20 to 24 is a nice range for the number of buffers for most applications. I use a 512K PC and set the buffers at 40. Using more than 40 buffers can adversely affect the performance of other programs.

For readers really interested in witnessing the handling of buffers and files first hand, I offer the following experiment.

Start up dBASE III. After the disk check has frustrated you and the program is finally running, type

```
SET ALTER TO TEST
SET ALTER ON
```

Now USE a database, preferably a small one (fewer than 20 fields). Type

```
DISP STAT
```

to make sure that ALTERNATE is ON and the alternate file is TEST.TXT, as shown in figure 2.2.

Now type

```
DISP STRUC
```

You should now have in your ALTERNATE file facsimiles of the DISP STAT screen and the DISP STRUC screen for the database in USE. Now type

```
SET ALTER OFF
TYPE TEST.TXT
```

More than likely, you get nothing. But you have the ALTERNATE ON, and the file is properly named. Don't fret. Type

```
QUIT
```

and wait until dBASE III says goodbye and you're back at the DOS prompt. Now type

```
TYPE TEST.TXT
```

Voila. End of experiment.

```
->DISP STAT

Currently selected database:
Select area -  1, Database in use: C:STUDENTS.dbf   Alias - STUDENTS

Press any key to continue...




Press any key to continue...

File search path:    C:\DBASES\D3\D3STUFF
Default disk drive: C:
ALTERNATE     - OFF  DEBUG       - OFF  ESCAPE     - ON   MENU       - OFF
BELL          - ON   DELETED     - OFF  EXACT      - OFF  PRINT      - OFF
CARRY         - OFF  DELIMITERS  - OFF  HEADING    - ON   SAFETY     - ON
CONFIRM       - OFF  DEVICE      - SCRN HELP       - ON   STEP       - OFF
CONSOLE       - ON   ECHO        - OFF  INTENSITY  - ON   TALK       - ON
UNIQUE        - OFF

Margin =      0

Function key  F1  - help;
Function key  F2  - assist;
Function key  F3  - list;
Function key  F4  - dir;
Function key  F5  - display structure;
Function key  F6  - display status;
Function key  F7  - display memory;
Function key  F8  - display;
Function key  F9  - append;
Function key  F10 - CHR(27);QUIT;

->
```

Fig. 2.2. Contents of the ALTERNATE file.

This is a prime example of how DOS handles both files and buffers. Inside dBASE, with SET ALTER ON, all the screen information first is sent to a buffer. Every once in a while the buffer fills with information and flushes itself to the ALTERNATE file (TEST.TXT in the experiment). The buffer is now empty and ready for the next set of screens.

However, in our experiment we don't give the buffer a chance to flush itself when we are in dBASE. QUITting dBASE forced dBASE to close all open files, one of which was the ALTERNATE file. Further, it forces DOS to purge all buffers. This flushing is standard operating procedure for DOS when it exits a program. The result is that DOS first flushes the buffers then dBASE closes the files. Thus the difference between a buffer and a file is dramatically demonstrated.

The magic has to do with the fact that dBASE III (usually) stores the ALTERNATE file text in a buffer until the buffer is full. Once the buffer is full, dBASE III writes that information to the disk file. By QUITting to the system, you can force dBASE to write the information to the disk.

Using the same procedure to experiment with different size buffers is also worthwhile. Putting

```
BUFFERS=80
```

in your CONFIG.SYS file and rebooting the machine gives you much smaller buffers than using 20 or even 40 buffers. The smaller buffers cause dBASE III to write the information to the ALTERNATE file more often than do fewer, hence larger, buffers.

So much for getting information from buffers to the disk. Now we consider the reverse process.

Retrieving Data from the Disk

The diagram in figure 2.3 is meant to be an example and is not a realistic representation of the way data is actually stored or retrieved. Imagine this illustration as part of a disk file containing data.

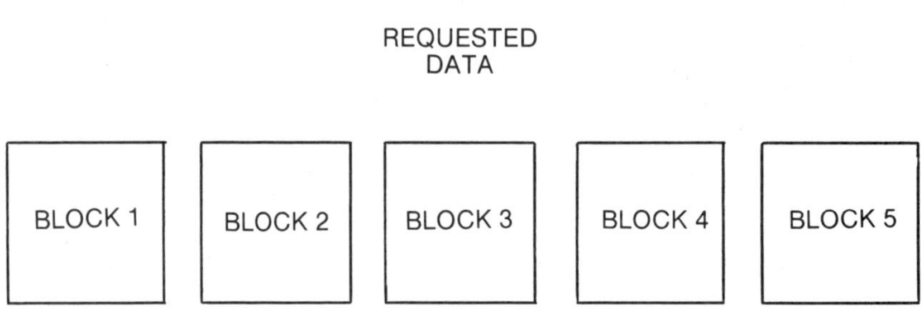

Fig. 2.3. Blocks of data in a disk file.

We are interested in accessing data block 3. When we are using the buffers created by the CONFIG.SYS file and we request block 3, we also pull into that buffer blocks 1, 2, 4, and 5. Why? Because somewhere along the development of the PC and DOS systems, someone decided that keeping information in buffers would be good. The point is not that buffers are new to the PC; all computers, from large mainframes to lowly 8-bit machines, use them. The point is that the information usually kept in those buffers is close (in the disk file) to the last information requested. The strength of the PC is that the algorithms for managing data in buffers are fairly sophisticated. The PC often employs a "most used" referencing algorithm that keeps in memory the data accessed most often.

Buffering information that is close to the last information requested makes sense if you're working with word-processing files or programs too large to fit into machine memory. Usually these applications get information in a linear fashion. (We look at the last paragraph, this paragraph, then the next paragraph, or we look at program line 2000, 2010, 2020, 2030 . . .). But we don't always the way we request information from a database in that order.

If you constantly reference block 3, you have no problem. That information is kept in a buffer close to the top of a stack of buffers. But now imagine you request information in block 10. DOS pushes down the block 3 information and places the block 10 information on top of the stack. Now you look at block 90. The stack, reading from the top down, becomes

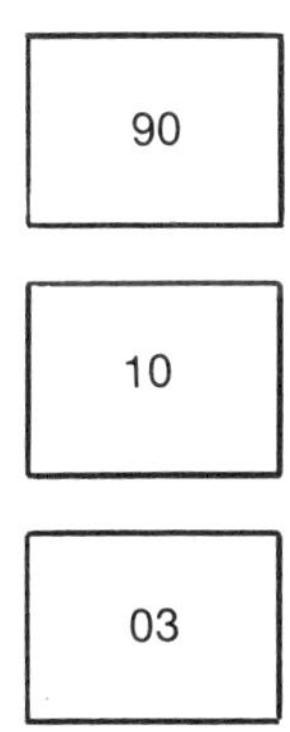

Now you want 3's information again and the stack shifts (it doesn't "pop") the block 3 information the top:

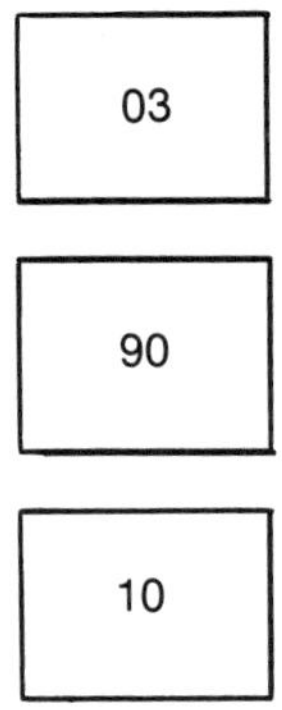

Suppose all 20 buffers get filled up. You're most often referencing data blocks 3, 90, 10, and 7, in that order, with block 82 referenced least often. The buffer stack looks like the following diagram:

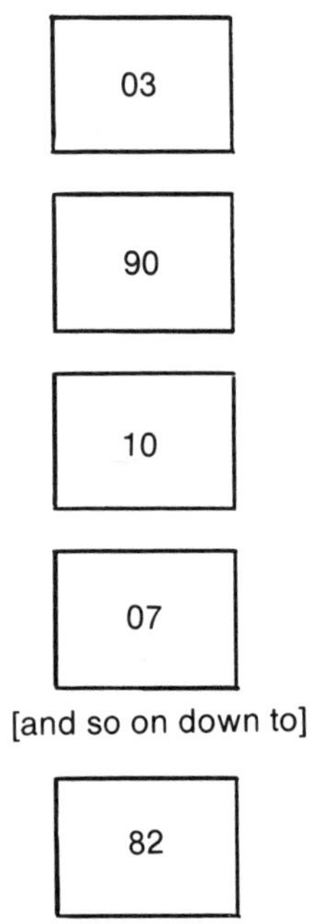

You now reference a new data block, 32, which has never been referenced before. Block 82's information gets "popped" off the bottom because 82 is the least used. The most used buffers stay in the buffer stack, with the most used closest to the top.

Keep this concept in mind when you are opening work areas and designing databases in dBASE III applications. The best uses of this concept can be seen in the sections on database templates and various types of data files.

Ram Disks, Virtual Disks, and dBASE III Files

Another way to solve the I/O problem is to use RAM-disk or V-disk software to create a high-speed drive, then copy everything needed to that drive. This practice has more advantages than the obvious ones.

As mentioned earlier, the dBASE programs are disk-based programs. Worse, they are interpreted at each run. This aspect of dBASE's design makes the computer run as fast as molasses flowing uphill in January. The smart use of RAM or V-disks therefore is not necessarily to use them for database files and their kin. Instead, it may be wiser to load your program and related files (rather than huge databases) in electronic disks, especially if your program is read more often than the database information. The data is stored and manipulated in buffers, but the code to execute the manipulations (a long DO WHILE . . . ENDDO, for example) is pulled from the disk each time that code is needed.

A combination of the two techniques—loading your program files into electronic disks and using only the necessary parts of a database—form an excellent method for keeping the end process clicking along at a good pace.

Physical Records

Place 100 folders containing information in a box. Pick up the folders one at a time. They are physical records. Now pretend the information in those 100 folders is in a dBASE III database file in the same sequence as in the folders. The records in the database file are still physical records. We call them *physical* because they are not *logical*, which is a word we reserve for discussions of random access.

The only thing really worth remembering about all this is that physical records are the actual records in the database. That's it, nothing more. The following is an example of a check register file. It is physical in that the checks are listed as they were written.

```
RECNO()          PAIDTO          AMOUNT

232              SEARS           $  59.95
233              MOBIL           $  22.75
234              CASH            $1000.00
235              MOBIL           $  30.00
236              CASH            $   5.00
237              SEARS           $  20.00
```

Sequential Access

When we access data one record after another—first, second, and so on to the last—we are sequentially accessing the data. That we don't do anything with the majority of the records makes no difference; all that matters is that we look at them one after the other.

Sequential access is another great time-eater in dBASE III programming. One reason is that sequential processing always uses disks; it doesn't involve buffers at all. When you use LOCATE or use a command with a FOR qualifier, for instance, get ready for a long wait because you are using sequential access.

One way to speed up LOCATEing records involves forethought—something I've said never goes well with programming.

We rely on the fact that no matter what anyone says, data is not random. No matter what kind of data is stored in the database, the actual data follows a bell curve. It may not follow a bell curve for the most significant INDEXed fields, but it definitely follows the curve on one if not several other fields. Examples of this are given in the sections on "Primary and Secondary Keys" and "Index Files and Bell Curves."

At times sequential access is the only way to go, but sequential access is best reserved for management rather than manipulations.

Management rather than manipulation? The difference concerns the size of the working database. We manage large DBF files. In other words, we have no intentions of making any changes directly to the files. What we do is look for information we need, bring that data to a smaller database file, and manipulate the data there. Database management, for the purposes of this book, can be likened to file management. Database manipulation is what I do when I alter records in a file.

Unless we are very careful in writing our files to disk, they are written in a hodgepodge sequential manner. And that aspect of file structure is the reason for separating files logically. Records are appended to a file as they are entered, with no order whatsoever. Consider the following data set:

City	*State*
Portsmouth	NH
Hanover	NH
Manchester	MA
Manchester	NH
Boston	MA
New Boston	NH
New Bedford	MA
Bedford	NH

This data set is appended, one record at a time, to a file containing the names of several other cities in New England.

City	*State*
Norwich	VT
Lebanon	NH
Burlington	VT
Keene	NH
Colebrook	NH
St. Johnsbury	VT
Brattleboro	VT

Readers who are familiar with New England will perceive some order in my listing, but that order results entirely from associations in my own mind; I listed the cities as I thought of them.

If the names of the cities are entered in the order in which they are listed, they go sequentially into the database.

City	*State*
Portsmouth	NH
Hanover	NH
Manchester	MA
Manchester	NH
Boston	MA
New Boston	NH
New Bedford	MA
Bedford	NH
Norwich	VT
Lebanon	NH

Burlington	VT
Keene	NH
Colebrook	NH
St. Johnsbury	VT
Brattleboro	VT

This data set has no order; we were not careful in entering data. Because we have little control on how data is sent to disk, we are not careful in writing our files to disk. The data is stored on disk as it was entered. The result is a data mess. And that is exactly how the data will be read back out: as a disorderly mess.

Logical Records

The term *logical* record implies that we, the humans who use the computer, have chosen some method of ordering physical records. We have chosen an INDEXing method.

For example, the check register data in the previous section consists of physical records. We make their order logical by grouping the records according to PAIDTO.

RECNO()	PAIDTO	AMOUNT
234	CASH	$1000.00
236	CASH	$ 5.00
233	MOBIL	$ 22.75
235	MOBIL	$ 30.00
232	SEARS	$ 59.95
237	SEARS	$ 20.00

We can be even fancier and order the list by PAIDTO and then by AMOUNT, in increasing order.

RECNO()	PAIDTO	AMOUNT
236	CASH	$ 5.00
234	CASH	$1000.00
233	MOBIL	$ 22.75
235	MOBIL	$ 30.00
237	SEARS	$ 20.00
232	SEARS	$ 59.95

We've taken items entered "at random" and arranged them according to some predetermined "logical" method.

Random Access

Now the question is, "What does *random* mean?" In this connection it means "highly ordered." No, I haven't been in the wine cellar too long. Random means taking things, one here, one there, one somewhere else. Consider the following sequence of random numbers:

01, 21, 30, 62, 67, 68, 70, 79, 80

Say these numbers represent record numbers in a database of 100 records. Further, say they represent the only records in our database that share some common bond. We INDEX on this common bond and behold! Our random sequence becomes highly ordered. We still pick one here, one there, one somewhere else. But now we're exact in what we pick from here, there, and elsewhere. So our random access is not so random. The order is definitely not sequential, however.

A truly random access occurs when we use LOCATE or a FOR condition. The records are read sequentially (in their physical order). The condition we're interested in occurs at random in the database.

Primary and Secondary Keys

The mechanism that orders our random access relies upon primary and secondary keys. A primary key is what the computer uses to keep track of where information is in a database. dBASE III uses record numbers—the RECNO( ) function—as a primary key for finding information.

This is all well and good for dBASE III, but not for us mortals. The secondary key is what we mortals can understand; it points to the primary key, which the computer can understand.

For instance, our checkbooks contain dates, check numbers, debit and credit information, balances, and descriptions: interest, activity charge, phone bill. When Sears says we didn't pay our bill, we look through our descriptions for references such as "SEARS." The references appear at random, and we order them with the index key

```
description="SEARS"
```

Once we've found all our "SEARS" descriptions, we note check numbers and amounts to inform Sears of the error. This example illustrates the use of primary (check number) and secondary (description="SEARS") keys.

More practical examples of the use of primary and secondary keys can be seen in the programs UPDATER.PRG (Chapter 5) and NEWUPDTR.PRG (Chapter 7). UPDATER.PRG uses sequential access; NEWUPDTR.PRG uses random access. Note that UPDATER.PRG uses a sequential (unINDEXed) file and examines each record FOR a condition. NEWUPDTR.PRG starts with a logically ordered file, FINDs the first record that meets our condition, then takes only those records that meet our condition. All records that match our condition are next to each other in a logically ordered file.

3
Subroutines and dBASE III PROCEDURE Files

A *subroutine* is a group of commands that the main program uses to perform a specific task. More precisely, a subroutine is a group of commands not needed every time the main program is executed; it is used only if certain conditions are met in the main body of the program. Menu systems are almost always subroutines of a central program. A good example of the use of subroutines is the front end system designed in Chapter 2, the Northeast Sales Main Menu. This system employs a central program that uses other modules to do tasks as needed.

The question arises as to whether some subroutines should be kept in the main body of the program. Well, yes; some subroutines are used so often that they should be in the main body of the program. But I also say to use modular coding, which produces many little files. Using small files can mean eating up a great deal of disk space and most certainly means more wear and tear for the disk and drive than is healthy for your computer system.

Fortunately, dBASE III has a way to solve this dilemma. The solution is dBASE III's PROCEDURE file. Before I talk about forming PROCEDURE files, I will describe how they work.

Assume you have a program called BLACKBOX. Inside the BLACKBOX is something called THRDSIDE, which determines the third side of a right triangle. When you give the program the measurements of two sides, it tells you the third. You don't care how THRDSIDE works; all you care about is the fact that when you supply the dimensions of two sides, THRDSIDE gives you the third. If THRDSIDE is a subroutine, THRDSIDE is outside of the BLACKBOX. If THRDSIDE is part of a PROCEDURE file, the routine never leaves the BLACKBOX.

Following are three ways to activate THRDSIDE:

English	dBASE III Subroutine	dBASE III PROCEDURE
Hey, THRDSIDE	PUBLIC SIDE3	SET PROC TO BLACKBOX
One side is 10 units.	SIDE1=10	SIDE1=10
The other is 20 units.	SIDE2=20	SIDE2=20
What's the third side?	SIDE3=0	SIDE3=0
	DO THRDSIDE	DO THRDSIDE WITH; SIDE1, SIDE2, SIDE3

At this point THRDSIDE does some juggling, comes up with an answer, and sends the answer back to you as SIDE3. Slick.

Notice that the dBASE III subroutine code looks very much like a simple subroutine call. Why do we use procedures rather than subroutines?

Suppose you are interested in several geometric oddities. You have a clutter of subroutines: THRDSIDE, ANGLE, CIRCLE, DIAMETER, RADIUS, ULNA, and so on. One program, GEOMETRY, uses these subroutines frequently. None of the subroutines is particularly large, so you string them together in a PROCEDURE file. The following code consists of the GEOMETRY.PRG file, which uses the subroutines, and the PROCEDURE file, which does the actual work.

```
***GEOMETRY.PRG FILE
***BY JOSEPH-DAVID CARRABIS
**
SET TALK OFF
SET PROCEDURE TO ODDITIES * ODDITIES.PRG IS A FILE CONTAINING OUR SUBROUTINES
CLEAR
TEXT
```

```
=====================================================================
||           PRESS A FUNCTION KEY TO ANSWER A QUESTION             ||
=====================================================================
||                                                                 ||
||                                                                 ||
||           F1 -> EXIT                                            ||
||           F2 -> CIRCLE RADIUS              (NEEDS AREA)         ||
||           F3 -> CIRCLE DIAMETER            (NEEDS PERIMETER)    ||
||           F4 -> CIRCLE PERIMETER           (NEEDS RADIUS)       ||
||           F5 -> RT TRIANGLE HYPOTENUSE     (NEEDS TWO SIDES)    ||
||           F6 -> RT TRIANGLE PERIMETER      (NEEDS TWO SIDES)    ||
||           F7 -> BOX AREA                   (NEEDS TWO SIDES)    ||
||           F8 -> BOX PERIMETER              (NEEDS TWO SIDES)    ||
||           F9 -> IS BOX A QUADRILATERAL?    (NEEDS ONE ANGLE)    ||
||           F10 -> I HATED GEOMETRY CLASS!   (NEEDS HELP)         ||
||                                                                 ||
=====================================================================
ENDTEXT
**
DO WHILE .T.
   WAIT ' ' TO KEY
   @ 18,0 CLEAR
   KEYVALUE=ASC(KEY)
**
   DO CASE
      CASE KEYVALUE<246
         CLOS PROC
         CANCEL
**
      CASE KEYVALUE=254
         INPU "CIRCLE AREA?" TO VALUE
         DO RADIUS WITH VALUE
**
      CASE KEYVALUE=253
         INPU "CIRCLE PERIMETER?" TO VALUE
         DO DIAMETER WITH VALUE
**
      CASE KEYVALUE=252
         INPU "CIRCLE RADIUS?" TO VALUE
         DO CPERIM WITH VALUE
**
      CASE KEYVALUE=251
```

```
          STORE Ø TO VALUE1, VALUE2, VALUE3
          DO THRDSIDE WITH VALUE1, VALUE2, VALUE3
          DO CLEARER WITH VALUE3
**
       CASE KEYVALUE=25Ø
          STORE Ø TO VALUE1, VALUE2, VALUE3
          DO TPERIM WITH VALUE1, VALUE2, VALUE3
**
       CASE KEYVALUE=249
          DO BOXAREA
**
       CASE KEYVALUE=248
          DO BPERIM
**
       CASE KEYVALUE=247
          DO QUAD
**
       OTHERWISE
          ? "YEAH,  BUT YOU REMEMBERED WHAT SHE TAUGHT YOU!"
   ENDCASE
ENDDO
CLOS PROC
**
***END OF GEOMETRY.PRG

***ODDITIES.PRG PROCEDURE FILE
***BY JOSEPH-DAVID CARRABIS,  AND SO ON AND SO FORTH
**
PROCEDURE CLEARER * TO DISPLAY THE ANSWER AND CLEAR THE SCREEN
PARAMETER ANSWER
@ 18,Ø CLEAR
@ 2Ø,Ø SAY "THE ANSWER IS "+STR(ANSWER,1Ø,5)
WAIT
@ 18,Ø CLEAR
RETURN
**
PROCEDURE RADIUS * RADIUS = PI*SQR(R)
PARAMETER AREA
RADIUS=SQRT(AREA/3.141)
DO CLEARER WITH RADIUS
RETURN
**
```

```
PROCEDURE DIAMETER * DIAMETER=2R=PERIMETER/PI
PARAMETER PERIMETER
DIAMETER=PERIMETER/3.141
DO CLEARER WITH DIAMETER
RETURN
**
PROCEDURE CPERIM * CIRCLE PERIMETER=2RPI
PARAMETER RADIUS
PERIMETER=RADIUS*6.282
DO CLEARER WITH PERIMETER
RETURN
**
PROCEDURE THRDSIDE * HYPOTENUSE=SQRT(SUM OF SQUARES OF SIDES)
PARAMETER SIDE1,SIDE2,SIDE3
INPU "WHAT IS SIDE 1? " TO SIDE1
INPU "WHAT IS SIDE 2? " TO SIDE2
SIDE3=SQRT(SIDE1*SIDE1+SIDE2*SIDE2)
RETURN
**
PROCEDURE TPERIM *
PARAMETER SIDE1,SIDE2,SIDE3
DO THRDSIDE WITH SIDE1,SIDE2,SIDE3
PERIMETER=SIDE1+SIDE2+SIDE3
DO CLEARER WITH PERIMETER
**
PROCEDURE BOXAREA * AREA=SIDE1*SIDE2
INPU "WHAT IS SIDE 1? " TO SIDE1
INPU "WHAT IS SIDE 2? " TO SIDE2
AREA=SIDE1*SIDE2
DO CLEARER WITH AREA
RETURN
**
PROCEDURE BPERIM * PERIMETER=2*(SIDE1+SIDE2)

INPU "WHAT IS SIDE 1? " TO SIDE1
INPU "WHAT IS SIDE 2? " TO SIDE2
PERIMETER=2*(SIDE1+SIDE2)
DO CLEARER WITH PERIMETER
RETURN
**
```

```
PROCEDURE QUAD * IF ANGLE<>90 DEGREES -> BOX IS NOT QUADRILATERAL
INPU "WHAT IS THE ANGLE (IN DEGREES)? " TO ANGLE
IF ANGLE<>90
   ? "NO, IT IS NOT."
ELSE
   ? "YES, IT IS."
ENDIF
WAIT
@ 19,0 CLEAR
RETURN
**
***END OF PROCEDURE FILE
```

You need to know why I choose to lump all these oddities into one PROCEDURE file and how using the PROCEDURE file helps dBASE III. First, all the oddities are small. Creating several subroutines would only tie up disk space and slow down the system with endless I/O. Second, this one large PROCEDURE file can be loaded into memory as one block of code and accessed from there. One disk access now handles the I/O for several subroutines.

Standards for Creating a PROCEDURE File

The requirements for setting up a PROCEDURE file are

1. All the subroutines should be short (3 to 50 lines of code).
2. The entire PROCEDURE file should comfortably fit in memory. (Determine the sizes of DOS and necessary dBASE III files, find out what is left over for your working files, and you'll have the size your PROCEDURE file should be. If you don't have a great deal of memory to play with, use subroutines. You'll be going to the disk no matter what.)
3. All the subroutines in the PROCEDURE file should be used frequently by the calling program during a session—either because a standard work session is long or because the files call each other.
4. You must have more than one subroutine. If not, include the one subroutine in the main body or leave the subroutine as a separately called program. It would be easier to code, anyway.

5. The maximum number of subroutines in a PROCEDURE file is 32.

The ODDITIES.PRG PROCEDURE file is set up following standard programming logic. The most frequently used subroutine, CLEARER, is at the top of the list. Repetitive questions (regarding triangles and boxes) are kept in the subroutines. We have no reason to weigh down the main body of the program with questions that might never be asked (if we were interested only in circles, for example). The other subroutines follow in the order on the calling menu.

Other Features of PROCEDURE Files

The preceding file is also an example of some other interesting features of PROCEDURE files. Notice that I don't always pass PARAMETERs to the subroutines. PROCEDURE-based subroutines don't always need to be handed a stick to be able to run their leg of the race. This flexibility is useful, but it demands a warning note:

> If a PROCEDURE-based subroutine is called at several different locations or by several different programs, the calling commands must all agree in the number of PARAMETERs being passed.

You cannot use the command

```
DO RADIUS
```

because PROCEDURE RADIUS wants to get

```
PARAMETER AREA
```

from the calling program. Likewise, if EXAMPLE is a PROCEDURE-based subroutine with the first line

```
PARAMETER ONE, TWO, THREE
```

the subroutine can't be called with any of the following:

```
DO EXAMPLE WITH 5
DO EXAMPLE WITH DUCK, SOUP
DO EXAMPLE WITH THE, ALLAN, BRADY, SHOW
```

The reason for this restriction is that none of these calls to EXAMPLE passes the correct number of PARAMETERS. A call that works is

```
DO EXAMPLE WITH CALVIN,KLEIN,JEANS
```

If dBASE can't find subroutines in the declared PROCEDURE file, it looks elsewhere. These subroutines can be passed values exactly like their PROCEDURE-file cousins; you must have a PARAMETER command as the first executable command in the subroutine.

Another point worth noting is that subroutines in PROCEDURE files can DO other subroutines in the same PROCEDURE file. Notice, for example, that CLEARER is accessed by most of the other subroutines in ODDITIES.

CLEARER is also the first subroutine in the file. This fact brings us to an interesting point. With many of the higher-level languages, programmers can define subroutines as procedures at the beginning of the main body of code. dBASE III is an exception to this rule in a certain sense: In dBASE III you cannot place PROCEDUREs directly before the working code in the main program. Doing so causes dBASE to exit the program as soon as it reaches the first PROCEDURE name in the list. Because dBASE III is interpreted one line at a time, placing PROCEDURES at the end of the main body of code is also out of the question.

However, you can design your PROCEDURE files to be recursive to themselves if the called PROCEDUREs are placed before the calling PROCEDUREs in the file. Proper design of these files can get you some highly memory-intensive programs that access the disk only at the start and end of a work session.

All the PROCEDURE files I've designed originated as a group of related subroutines. The main menu system developed earlier in this book shows a group of jobs performed by similar tasks. Each task is a subroutine that performs a specific function. Once the separate subroutines are debugged and functional, I revise that menu and code to create the following:

```
SET PROC TO FROMFRST
DO WHILE .T.
CHOICE=0
CLEAR
TEXT
```

```
======================================================================
||     N O R T H E A S T   S A L E S   M A I N   M E N U        ||
======================================================================
||                                                                  ||
||                                                                  ||
||            Ø. Exit                                               ||
||            1. Customer Mailing List                              ||
||            2. Factory Totals by Month and Year                   ||
||            3. Customer Totals by Month and Year                  ||
||            4. Commission Report                                  ||
||            5. Unpaid Commission Report                           ||
||            6. Factory Listing                                    ||
||            7. Active Customer Listing                            ||
||            8. Inactive Customer Listing                          ||
||            9. Update Customers                                   ||
||           1Ø. Update Factories                                   ||
||           11. Update Items Sold                                  ||
||           12. Update Salespeople                                 ||
||           13. Back Up All Files                                  ||
||           14. Retrieve All Files                                 ||
||                                                                  ||
=========================Your Choice -> == <-=========================
   ENDTEXT
   @ 22,44 GET CHOICE PICTURE "##"
   READ
*
   DO CASE
      CASE CHOICE=Ø
         RETURN
*
      CASE CHOICE=1
         DO MAILLIST WITH CUSTOMERS
*
      CASE CHOICE=2
         DO TOTALS WITH FACTORY
*
      CASE CHOICE=3
         DO TOTALS WITH CUSTOMER
*
      CASE CHOICE<6
         DO COMMRPRT
*
      CASE CHOICE=6
```

```
         DO LISTINGS WITH FACTORY
*
      CASE CHOICE<9
         DO LISTINGS WITH CUSTOMER
*
      CASE CHOICE=9
         DO MAIN WITH CUSTOMER
*
      CASE CHOICE=10
         DO MAIN WITH FACTORY
*
      CASE CHOICE=11
         DO MAIN WITH ITEMSOLD
*
      CASE CHOICE=12
         DO MAIN WITH SALESTAF
*
      CASE CHOICE=13
         RUN BACKUP
*
      CASE CHOICE=14
         RUN RESTORE
*
      OTHERWISE
         WAIT "Valid Choices are 0-14. Press any key to continue."
   ENDCASE
*
ENDDO
```

The PROCEDURE file, FROMFRST.PRG, looks like this:

```
***PROCEDURE FILE FROMFRST.PRG
***BY JOSEPH-DAVID CARRABIS ETC.
**
PROCEDURE MAIN
PARAMETER FILENAME
USE &FILENAME INDE &FILENAME

     [code for MAIN subroutine]

RETURN
**
PROCEDURE LISTINGS
PARAMETER FILENAME
USE &FILENAME INDE &FILENAME
```

```
     [code for LISTINGS subroutine]

RETURN
**
PROCEDURE TOTALS
PARAMETER FILENAME
USE &FILENAME INDE &FILENAME

     [code for TOTALS subroutine]

RETURN
**
PROCEDURE MAILLIST
PARAMETER FILENAME
USE &FILENAME INDE &FILENAME

     [code for MAILLIST subroutine]

RETURN
**
***END OF FROMFRST PROCEDURE FILE
```

Again notice that I followed the logic of tasks, and I gave the problem some forethought. Extra menu selections can be added without changing the PROCEDURE file. BACKUP.PRG and RESTORE.PRG files are not included in the PROCEDURE file because they do not follow one of the rules dictating the inclusion of a subroutine in such a file—that is, they are not called frequently during a session.

The RUN Command

The philosophy presented in the preceding section has been to put complete and repeatedly called dBASE III subroutines in a PROCEDURE file. And, in this sentence, I added an implication not mentioned earlier.

The implication is in the four words "repeatedly called dBASE III." Subroutines that are repeatedly called should be placed in PROCEDURE files.

But what about modules that are only called once a while and are not coded in dBASE III? How can we utilize a MASM file that is only needed at startup, perhaps to change the access codes of some files?

dBASE III has a powerful command that many programmers fail to use: the RUN command. Many experienced dBASE II programmers have suffered because they have overlooked that command. But those dBASE II programmers who used

```
QUIT TO "COMFILE1", "COMFILE2",...
```

will definitely use

```
RUN COMFILE1
RUN COMFILE2
    .
    .
    .
```

The only problem is that to RUN anything requires more than 256K of main memory. Many utilities, including DOS, can be run if you are using 320K. The advantages are immediately obvious once you realize that instead of coding

```
COPY FILE filename.ext TO DN:filename.ext
```

you only have to code

```
RUN COPY filename.ext DN:
```

(DN: designates Drive Name in these examples.)

The power of RUN is that we can access subroutines that are not dBASE III subroutines just as if they were part of the dBASE III system. What might we use such subroutines for?

Typically, I use subroutines that are not dBASE III to determine available disk space before I attempt to write files. I use these subroutines for data and program encryption and decryption, for running DOS BACKUP and RESTORE programs, for word processors, for spreadsheets, and so on.

I did not include CHOICES 13 and 14 of my MAINMENU in my FROMFRST PROCEDURE file. Such mass backup and restore functions are already handled well by DOS programs. We don't need to recode them because no one expects us to reinvent the wheel. (Advanced programmers never work harder than they have to.) Hence, the end of the main menu can take one of two forms, depending on whether I have a hard disk system or dual floppies.

```
                    HARD DISK SYSTEM METHOD

CASE CHOICE=13
RUN BACKUP * YOU CAN ALSO INCLUDE APPROPRIATE SWITCHES
CASE CHOICE=14
RUN RESTORE
ENDCASE

                    DUAL FLOPPY DISK METHOD

CASE CHOICE<=14
MORE=.T.
DO WHILE MORE
RUN DISKCOPY A: B:
CLEAR
INPU "DO ANOTHER (Y/N)? " TO MORE
ENDDO
ENDCASE
```

The point is simple enough: the more you use a piece of code, the more accessible it is to the main program (see fig. 3.1).

In all likelihood, the only COM or EXE files you use in your application are either utilities you've written or non-dBASE applications (word processor, telecommunications, spreadsheet). These applications will not be called often during a work session, so you need only to RUN them.

Next in ease of access are modules that can be coded in dBASE III, but are not called often—for example, a module that checks each database for deleted or altered records, then makes backup databases and packs the working databases. These functions can be written in dBASE III syntax, but are used once (if at all) during a work session. These modules are summoned from the main body by a DO.

Modules that are not necessary for the function of the main program as a whole but are necessary to specific elements of the main program are placed in PROCEDURE files. Such a procedure file might contain modules that call up HELP files or redefine function keys. These modules are not important to the working of the main program, but are necessary for you to be able to work with the main program.

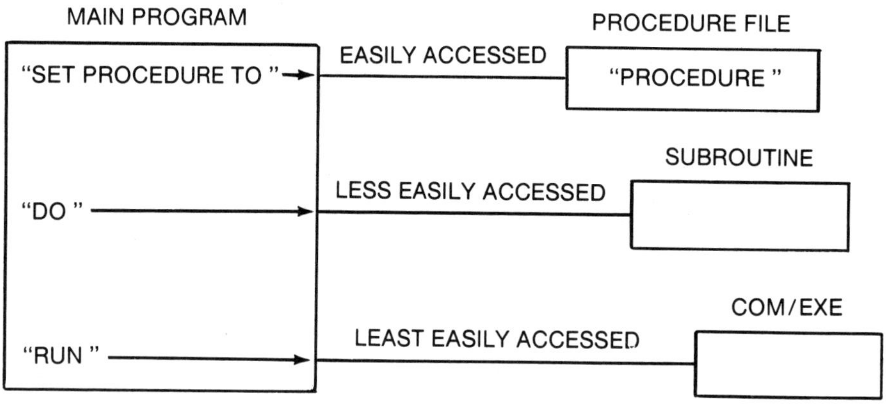

Fig. 3.1. Accessibility of code from the main program.

4
Coding in Modules

What does it mean to code in modules, and who is Dijkstra, anyway?

Starting with E. W. Dijkstra. He "invented" structured programming, a practice I hammer into my students and strive for in my own work. So much for Dijkstra, let's talk about structured programming.

Doing Structured Programming

Structured programming is also called top-down programming. Use either term; both terms mean that you code in tasks. If the fact that I'm talking about tasks is a surprise to you, well, you probably did as well in college as I did.

My flowcharts begin pretty much like anything else—they're nebulous. They don't stay that way for long, however. As soon as I have a good idea of what has to be done, I write the flowchart. It shows me what tasks need to be done.

Organizing the Program

Now comes the real work. Now comes top-down programming.

We take each task separately. The main menu of the program presented in Chapter 2 shows seven tasks needed to do fourteen jobs. Let's look at the database access module. Forget the other modules for now; we are going to concentrate on one task: database access.

Ask yourself this question: Given a database, what operations would you do on it? You may have answers like

Edit specific records
Find specific records by a key
Locate anything
Move forward and backward
Replace selected fields in selected common records
Display data
Report data
Delete records
Pack the database

You may think of other options, but these seem enough to me. Let's code what we have thus far but not worry about writing perfect dBASE III code. We can make the code perfect after we have the idea in a logical form.

```
GET RESPONSE
    IF RESPONSE=EDIT
       GOTO RECORD TO EDIT
       EDIT
    IF RESPONSE=FIND
       GET KEY
       FIND KEY
    IF RESPONSE=LOCATE
       GET FIELDNAME AND VALUE
       LOCATE FIELDNAME FOR VALUE
       WHILE NOT EOF
             LOCATE AGAIN? -> YES => CONTINUE
                           -> NO  => EXIT WHILE
       END WHILE
    IF RESPONSE=MOVE
       FORWARD OR BACK?
          SKIP AS INDICATED
```

```
IF RESPONSE=REPLACE
   ALL OR NEXT N?
   GET FIELDNAME AND VALUE
   REPLACE [NEXT N] FIELDNAME WITH VALUE
IF RESPONSE=DISPLAY
   DISPLAY WHAT?
   DISPLAY
IF RESPONSE=REPORT
   REPORT TO PRINTER OR SCREEN?
   CONDITION?
      REPORT [FOR CONDITION] TO [PRINTER OR SCREEN]
IF RESPONSE=DELETE
   DELETE WHAT
   FOR, WHILE, NEXT N?
IF FOR/WHILE GET CONDITION
   DELETE [NEXT N] [FOR/WHILE [CONDITION]]
IF RESPONSE=PACK
   PACK
```

One item is missing from our logical form: We haven't mentioned our database. We move through the database and manipulate it, but we don't declare it. Very well, the top of our logical form can include the lines

```
USE DATABASE
PUT INFORMATION ON SCREEN
```

Writing the dBASE III Code

The logical form of the code is complete. Now we take this logical form and transform it into a dBASE III structure.

```
**ACCESS.PRG
**
LOGICAL=.T.
USE &DATABASE INDE &DATABASE
GOTO TOP
CLEAR
DO &FRAMER
**
```

```
DO WHILE .T.
   VALUE=SPACE(40)
   DO &GETTER
   CLEAR GETS
   @ 20,0 CLEAR
   WAIT "Your choice (any other key to exit) -> " TO RESPONSE
   RESPONSE=ASC(RESPONSE)
**
   DO CASE
      CASE RESPONSE<240
         RETURN
      CASE RESPONSE=254
         @ 20,0 CLEAR
         @ 21,0 SAY "How far (use '-n' to go backward) -> " GET VALUE
         READ
         SKIP VAL(VALUE)
      CASE RESPONSE=253
         @ 20,0 CLEAR
         @ 21,0 SAY "&KEYFIELD = " GET VALUE
         READ
         FIND &VALUE
      CASE RESPONSE=252
        @ 20,0 CLEAR
        @ 21,0 SAY "Locate expression ->  " GET VALUE
         READ
         SET INDE TO
         LOCATE FOR &VALUE
         DO WHILE .NOT. EOF()
            DO &GETTER
            CLEAR GETS
            RECNUM=RECNO()
            @ 23,0 SAY "Continue (Y/N)? " GET LOGICAL
            READ
            IF LOGICAL
               CONTINUE
            ELSE
               EXIT
            ENDIF
         ENDDO
         SET INDE TO &DATABASE
         GOTO RECNUM
```

```
      CASE RESPONSE=251
         DO &GETTER
         READ
      CASE RESPONSE=250
         @ 20,0 CLEAR
         ACCEPT "What field? " TO FIELDTYPE
         ACCEPT "Change it to? " TO NEWDATA
@ 23,0 SAY "(A)ll, (F)or condition, or number of records to replace -> ";
         GET VALUE
         READ
         DO CASE
            CASE UPPER(VALUE)="A"
               REPLACE ALL &FIELDTYPE WITH "&NEWDATA"
            CASE UPPER(VALUE)="F"
               ACCE "Condition -> " TO CONDITION
               REPLACE ALL &FIELDTYPE WITH "&NEWDATA" FOR &CONDITION
            CASE ASC(VALUE)<58
               REPLACE NEXT VAL(VALUE) &FIELDTYPE WITH "&NEWDATA"
         ENDCASE
      CASE RESPONSE=249
         @ 20,0 CLEAR
         ACCE "What fields (separate fields with ',')? " TO FIELDTYPE
@ 22,0 SAY "(A)ll, (F)or condition, or number of records to display -> ";
         GET VALUE
         READ
         DO CASE
            CASE UPPER(VALUE)="A"
               DISPLAY ALL &FIELDTYPE
            CASE UPPER(VALUE)="F"
               ACCE "Condition -> " TO CONDITION
               DISPLAY ALL &FIELDTYPE FOR &CONDITION
            CASE ASC(VALUE)<58
               DISPLAY NEXT VAL(VALUE) &FIELDTYPE
         ENDCASE
         WAIT
         CLEAR
         DO &FRAMER
      CASE RESPONSE=248
         @ 20,0 CLEAR
```

```
@ 21,0 SAY "(A)ll, (F)or condition, or number of records to report -> ";
          GET VALUE
          READ
          ACCE "Print or screen (type word)? " TO PORS
          ACCE "Report form name? " TO FORMTYPE
          DO CASE
             CASE UPPER(VALUE)="A"
                REPORT FORM &FORMTYPE TO &PORS
             CASE UPPER(VALUE)="F"
                ACCE "Condition -> " TO CONDITION
                REPORT FORM &FORMTYPE FOR &CONDITION TO &PORS
             CASE ASC(VALUE)<58
                REPORT FORM &FORMTYPE NEXT VAL(VALUE) TO &PORS
          ENDCASE
          WAIT
          CLEAR
          DO &FRAMER
       CASE RESPONSE=247
          @ 20,0 CLEAR
@ 21,0 SAY "(A)ll, (F)or condition, or number of records to delete -> ";
          GET VALUE
          READ
          DO CASE
             CASE UPPER(VALUE)="A"
                DELE ALL
             CASE UPPER(VALUE)="F"
                ACCE "Condition -> " TO CONDITION
                DELE ALL FOR &CONDITION
             CASE ASC(VALUE)<58
                DELE NEXT VAL(VALUE)
          ENDCASE
       CASE RESPONSE=246
          COPY TO TEMP
          USE TEMP
          COPY TO &DATABASE
          INDEX ON &KEYFIELD TO &DATABASE
          USE &DATABASE INDE &DATABASE
   ENDCASE
ENDDO
```

A nice feature of the preceding routine is that it uses the function keys in the tried-and-true way of capturing the key value with a WAIT TO command. Readers may not be aware of this technique, so allow me this little digression.

The WAIT command in dBASE III can be used to input single-character data into the program. Any character can be received, including graphics characters and those associated with the function keys and control keys. In the preceding listing, I've used the WAIT command in this way to capture the values of the function keys, which I have redefined for my own purposes.

Note that the routine doesn't include any error-checking procedure. Because that element is omitted, no attempt is made to prevent screen scrolling. Normally, I SET TALK OFF to prevent dBASE III from telling me what it's doing and to suppress error messages. The preceding code doesn't provide a means of catching errors via loops or traps; I therefore chose to leave TALK ON.

Now let's check to see whether anything else is missing. Particularly, we must make sure each variable is either declared or passed. We find that the variables DATABASE, KEYFIELD, FRAMER, and GETTER are used but neither declared nor passed.

We have two useful methods for declaring and passing variables. First, we can include

```
PARAMETER DATABASE, KEYFIELD
```

in our module (read task) and use

```
DO db3-30.db3 WITH DATABASE, KEYFIELD
```

or

```
DO db3-60.db3 WITH "database name", "keyfield name"
```

when we call the module. Second, we can simply declare

```
PUBLIC DATABASE, KEYFIELD
DATABASE="database name"
KEYFIELD="keyfield name"
```

before we call the subroutine.

What else is missing? We haven't described our FRAMER and GETTER modules. They are also subroutines, and their names are based on our database. For instance, if our database is called CLIENTS, our framer file could be called CLIENTS.FRA and our getter file could be CLIENTS.GET. We can build them off our DATABASE variable using the commands

```
FRAMER=DATABASE+".FRM"GETTER=DATABASE+".GET"
```

We also need to let our users know what the function keys do. (Key functions for a general-purpose database are given in Chapter 11.) I use the screen shown in figure 4.1.

```
================================================================================================
!! F1 = EXIT   !                                                                              !!
!! F2 = SKIP   !                                                                              !!
!! F3 = FIND   !                                                                              !!
!! F4 = LCTE   !                                                                              !!
!! F5 = EDIT   !                                                                              !!
!! F6 = RPLC   !                                                                              !!
!! F7 = DISP   !                                                                              !!
!! F8 = RPRT   !                                                                              !!
!! F9 = DELE   !                                                                              !!
!! F0 = PACK   !                                                                              !!
!!------------ !                                                                              !!
!!DATABASE =   !                                                                              !!
!!>DATABASE    !                                                                              !!
!!             !                                                                              !!
!!KEYFIELD =   !                                                                              !!
!!>KEYFIELD    !                                                                              !!
!!             !                                                                              !!
================================================================================================
->
->
->
->
->
```

Fig. 4.1. A screen display showing key functions.

Although it looks like a time-consuming endeavor, this screen is easily generated with the SED utility. The screen is transformed into this code:

```
CLEAR
@ Ø,1 SAY "===========================
============================"
@ Ø,56 SAY "========================"
@ 1,1 SAY "|| F1 = EXIT |"
@ 1,78 SAY "||"
@ 2,1 SAY "|| F2 = SKIP |"
@ 2,78 SAY "||"
@ 3,1 SAY "|| F3 = FIND |"
```

```
@ 3,78 SAY "||"
@ 4,1 SAY "|| F4 = LCTE |"
@ 4,78 SAY "||"
@ 5,1 SAY "|| F5 = EDIT |"
@ 5,78 SAY "||"
@ 6,1 SAY "|| F6 = RPLC |"
@ 6,78 SAY "||"
@ 7,1 SAY "|| F7 = DISP |"
@ 7,78 SAY "||"
@ 8,1 SAY "|| F8 = RPRT |"
@ 8,78 SAY "||"
@ 9,1 SAY "|| F9 = DELE |"
@ 9,78 SAY "||"
@ 1Ø,1 SAY "|| FØ = PACK |"
@ 1Ø,78 SAY "||"
@ 11,1 SAY "||-----------|"
@ 11,78 SAY "||"
@ 12,1 SAY "||DATABASE=  |"
@ 12,78 SAY "||"
@ 13,1 SAY "||"
@ 13,4 SAY DATABASE
@ 13,14 SAY "|"
@ 13,78 SAY "||"
@ 14,1 SAY "||           |"
@ 14,78 SAY "||"
@ 15,1 SAY "||KEYFIELD=  |"
@ 15,78 SAY "||"
@ 16,1 SAY "||"
@ 16,4 SAY KEYFIELD
@ 16,14 SAY "|"
@ 16,78 SAY "||"
@ 17,1 SAY "||           |"
@ 17,78 SAY "||"
@ 18,1 SAY "===========================
==========================="
@ 18,56 SAY "========================"
```

When using a box screen for database access, we naturally have to make sure our data fits. The box parameters give us a square with corners at screen coordinates (0,1), (0,80), (18,1) and (18,80). We can easily fit a "personality profile" FRAMER into this area (see fig. 4.2).

```
                First Name:
                Last Name :

                City      :                                        State:
                                                                   Zip   :

                Age             :
                Profession      :
                Hobby           :
                Last Book Read  :
                Latest Acoomplishment:
                Why they do what they do:
                Quote           :
                Profile         :
                Their Scotch    :
->
->
->
->
->
```

Fig. 4.2. A "profile" FRAMER.

The FRAMER can be coded as follows:

```
CLEAR
@ 2,16 SAY "First Name:"
@ 3,16 SAY "Last Name :"
@ 5,16 SAY "City      :                                   State:"
@ 6,60 SAY "ZIP  :"
@ 8,16 SAY "Age            :"
@ 9,16 SAY "Profession     :"
@ 10,16 SAY "Hobby           :"
@ 11,16 SAY "Last Book Read:"
@ 12,16 SAY "Latest Accomplishment:"
@ 13,16 SAY "Why they do what they do:"
@ 14,16 SAY "Quote           :"
@ 15,16 SAY "Profile         :"
```

The GETTER can be similarly coded.

How does the access module come together? If we are using the CUSTOMER database, we have

```
DATABASE="CUSTOMER"
DO DBACCESS
```

Our work on the database access module is complete. Now we can move on to the other modules.

Tracing the Logic

Let's look at what we did. We did top-down, or structured, programming. Our logic followed this path:

1. We defined the problem.
2. We broke the problem into modules.
3. We defined the modules.
4. We broke the modules into their constituent modules.
5. We coded the constituents.
6. We ran the constituents and debugged them as necessary.
7. We coded only what was necessary to maintain our task philosophy.
8. We ran the mo and debugged them as necessary.
9. We coded the problem.
10. We linked, or chained, the modules together.
11. We ran the program and debugged as necessary.
12. We were done.

Two new terms appear in step 10: *link* and *chain*. Readers with assembly language or compiler backgrounds now nod knowingly; others pale. No need. dBASE III makes linking and chaining simple.

Linking simply means that we get all the separate pieces together in the most logical way possible. Usually we link programs in the order that we use them. Linking in that way can be difficult, however, if some subroutines are called repeatedly; the result is spaghetti code. PROCEDURE files simplify linking to some extent. Repeatedly accessed subroutines are identified by SET PROCEDURE TO.

Chaining describes the method that structured programs use: only one part of the program—the necessary part—is in memory at any time. Getting the parts into memory when needed is quite simple: tell dBASE III to DO something. The PRG file that is the object of the DO is then loaded into memory. Normally a pointer of some kind is placed in the calling program so that dBASE "knows" where to return to.

If you are chaining, you might write a top-level file like this:

```
*** TOP LEVEL PRG FILE
***
DO PROGNUM1
DO PROGNUM2
DO PROGNUM3
DO PROGNUM4
 ...
 ...
```

Structured programming gets us into the habit of modular coding. We code in specific groups. The database access module, DBACCESS, is now a task-oriented module that can be used for many of our database tasks. Likewise, our other task-oriented modules, LISTING, MAILLIST, and so on, can be used for a wide variety of purposes.

The following sections deal with the concept of modular coding in more detail.

Combining the Subroutines

I've spent many words telling you how subroutines can help and hurt a dBASE III program (see "Subroutines and dBASE III PROCEDURE Files" in Chapter 3). I've discussed memory, file and buffer size, disk I/O, and other topics, all pertaining to the efficient use of memory space, disk space, and files. This section and the next are the beginning of the return on our investment. We're going to start hoarding our solutions.

Let's consider an inventory system as an example. Any inventory system will do, and I mean that literally. All inventory systems share many characteristics. Part number, part description, quantity in stock, cost per item, total inventory value, and reorder level are practically universal to inventory systems.

Next, we consider what operations are likely to be performed on an inventory. We do our standard manipulations—edit, delete, display, add, and so on—but we also do things unique to inventories, such as

Print purchases
Update inventory as purchases are made
Print stock report (what's moving, what's not, what's left)

These procedures form a fairly complete program for all inventory systems. Well, not quite. What we have mentioned can definitely be used by all inventory systems. Users of larger inventory systems, however, are also interested in location of stock (warehouse number or city) and reorder quantity; and they may need to break out the stock price into a separate database containing price and quantity-discount information.

Our interest here, however, is in the core programs necessary to all inventory systems. We use the INVENTORY database, which is structured as follows:

```
Structure for database    : C:INVENTORY.DBF
Number of data records    : 4
Date of last update       : 07/02/85

Field  Field name     Type        Width  Dec
  1    PARTNUM        Character     10
  2    DESCRPTION     Character     30
  3    INSTOCK        Numeric       10     2
  4    UNITS          Character      5
  5    PERITEM        Numeric       10     2
  6    TOTALVALUE     Numeric       10     2
  7    ORDERLEVEL     Numeric       10     2

** Total **                         86
```

We also use the database PRINTPLT for printing the total customer order. PRINTPLT is structured as follows:

```
Structure for database    : C:PRINTPLT.DBF
Number of data records    : 0
Date of last update       : 07/02/85

Field  Field name     Type        Width  Dec
  1    DESCRPTION     Character     20
  2    QUANT          Numeric       10     2
  3    PARTNUM        Character     10
  4    DISCNT         Numeric       10     2
  5    SUBTTL         Numeric       10     2

** Total **                         61
```

And, of course, we need the programs that put the subroutines all together. In this case, I've created a menu file that calls up our different routines, one of which also calls up a PROCEDURE file with the necessary subroutines for the ordering screen (see fig. 4.3).

```
==========================================================================
!!               !                                                      !!
!! F7 = MTNC     ! INVENTORY DATABASE MANAGEMENT (ADD,DELETE,VIEW,ETC)  !!
!!               !                                                      !!
!! F8 = ORDR     ! ENTER CUSTOMER ORDERS AND PRINT SALES FORM           !!
!!               !                                                      !!
!! F9 = EOD      ! GENERATE END OF DAY REPORTS                          !!
!!               !                                                      !!
!! F0 = EXIT     ! RETURN TO WHATEVER                                   !!
==========================================================================

->
->
->
->
->
->
->
```

Fig. 4.3. A menu for calling up subroutines and procedures.

The screen directs the user to press the function key corresponding to the required activity. Typing F7 will cause the user to enter the database access module, DBACCESS. Note that in the following code, which generates the screen and WAITs for a response, I again use the WAIT command to capture a keystroke and place it into a variable.

```
**INVMAIN.PRG
**
@ 1,1 SAY "======================================================="
@ 1,56 SAY "======================="
@ 2,1 SAY "||             |"
@ 2,77 SAY "||"
@ 3,1 SAY "||F7 = MTNC | INVENTORY DATABASE MANAGEMENT (ADD,DELETE"
@ 3,56 SAY ",VIEW,ETC)              ||"
@ 4,1 SAY "||             |"
@ 4,77 SAY "||"
@ 5,1 SAY "||F8 = ORDR | ENTER CUSTOMER ORDERS AND PRINT SALES FOR"
@ 5,56 SAY "M                       ||"
@ 6,1 SAY "||             |"
```

```
@ 6,77 SAY "||"
@ 7,1 SAY "||F9 = EOD  | GENERATE END OF DAY REPORTS"
@ 7,77 SAY "||"
@ 8,1 SAY "||          |"
@ 8,77 SAY "||"
@ 9,1 SAY "||FØ = EXIT | RETURN TO WHATEVER"
@ 9,77 SAY "||"
@ 1Ø,1 SAY "======================================================="
@ 1Ø,56 SAY "======================="
**
WAIT "TYPE THE FUNCTION KEY OF YOUR CHOICE " TO RESPONSE
RESPONSE=ASC(RESPONSE)
IF RESPONSE>249 .OR. RESPONSE<=246
   RETURN
ENDIF
**
DO CASE
   CASE RESPONSE=248
      DO ORDER
   CASE RESPONSE=249
      DO DBACCESS
   CASE RESPONSE=247
      ? "PLEASE MAKE SURE THE PAPER AND THE PRINTER ARE READY"
      WAIT
      USE INVENTORY INDE PARTNUM
      REPORT FORM EOD1 NOEJECT TO PRINT
      REPORT FORM EOD2 FOR INSTOCK<ORDERLEVEL TO PRINT
ENDCASE

**ORDER.PRG FILE FOR INVENTORY CONTROL
**
SET PROCEDURE TO ORDRFILE
SELE D
USE PRINTPLT
SELE A
USE INVENTORY INDE PARTNUM
AGAIN=.T.
DO ORDRFMT
DO WHILE AGAIN
   SELE A
   STORE Ø TO QUANTITY,DISCOUNT,SUBTOTAL
   PN=SPACE(1Ø)
   DESCRIPTION=SPACE(3Ø)
```

```
@ 15,0 CLEAR
@ 20,10 SAY "Part Number -> " GET PN PICTURE "XXXXXXXXXX"
@ 22,10 SAY "Description -> " GET DESCRIPTION
READ
DO CASE
   CASE PN <> ' '
      SET INDEX TO PARTNUM
      FIND &PN
      IF EOF().AND.PN<>PARTNUM
         SET COLOR TO 7*
         @ 15,0 SAY "ITEM NOT FOUND"
         WAIT
         SET COLOR TO W, ,
         LOOP
      ENDI
   CASE DESCRIPTION <> ' '
      SET INDEX TO DESCRIPT
      FIND &DESCRIPTION
      IF EOF().AND. DESCRIPTION<>DESCRPTION
         SET COLOR TO 7*
         @ 15,0 SAY "ITEM NOT FOUND"
         WAIT
         SET COLOR TO W, ,
         LOOP
      ENDI
   OTHE
      SET COLOR TO 7*
      @ 15,0 SAY "Part Number and/or Description missing"
      WAIT
      SET COLOR TO W,
      LOOP
ENDC
DO ORDRGET WITH QUANTITY,DISCOUNT,SUBTOTAL
READ
REPLACE INSTOCK WITH INSTOCK-QUANTITY,TOTALVALUE WITH PERITEM*INSTOCK
SELE D
APPEND BLANK
REPLACE DESCRPTION WITH A->DESCRPTION,SUBTTL WITH SUBTOTAL,;
        QUANT WITH QUANTITY,PARTNUM WITH A->PARTNUM;
        DISCNT WITH DISCOUNT
@ 23,0 SAY "Order again? " GET AGAIN
READ
```

```
ENDDO
DO PRINTPLT

**ORDRFILE.PRG PROCEDURE FILE FOR INVENTORY DATABASE
PROCEDURE ORDRFMT
CLEAR
@ 1,1 SAY "======================================================="
@ 1,56 SAY "========================"
@ 2,1 SAY "||"
@ 2,78 SAY "||"
@ 3,1 SAY "||  Part Number :"
@ 3,78 SAY "||"
@ 4,1 SAY "||"
@ 4,78 SAY "||"
@ 5,1 SAY "||  Description :"
@ 5,78 SAY "||"
@ 6,1 SAY "||"
@ 6,78 SAY "||"
@ 7,1 SAY "||  (Quantity     x       Unit Cost)   -   Discount(%)  ="
@ 7,61 SAY "         Total     ||"
@ 8,1 SAY "||"
@ 8,78 SAY "||"
@ 9,1 SAY "||"
@ 9,78 SAY "||"
@ 10,1 SAY "======================================================="
@ 10,56 SAY "========================"
RETURN
**
PROCEDURE ORDRGET
PARA QUANTITY,DISCOUNT,SUBTOTAL
@ 3,19 SAY PARTNUM
@ 5,19 SAY DESCRPTION
@ 9,3 SAY SPACE(76)
@ 9,6 GET QUANTITY
@ 9,28 SAY PERITEM
@ 9,44 GET DISCOUNT PICTURE "999"
READ
DISCOUNT=(PERITEM*DISCOUNT)/100
SUBTOTAL=QUANTITY*(PERITEM-DISCOUNT)
@ 9,44 SAY DISCOUNT PICTURE "99999999.99"
@ 9,62 SAY SUBTOTAL PICTURE "99999999.99"
RETURN
**
```

```
PROCEDURE PRINTPLT
SELE D
SET FILTER TO TRIM(DESCRPTION) <> ' 'CLEAR
CLEAR
ACCE "Customer Name     -> " TO NAME
ACCE "Customer Address -> " TO ADDRESS
ACCE "City, State, ZIP -> " TO CSZ
WAIT "LINE UP THE PAPER AND TYPE ANY KEY WHEN READY"
REPORT FORM PRINTPLT NOEJECT TO PRINT
EJECT
ZAP
SET FILTER TO
RETURN
```

Now we have an inventory-control and order-entry system. Simple, neat. We already have our basic database access module (see Appendix D). We link the modules with the menu file, again using the function keys and some parameter passing. Linking modules with the menu makes them more universal than unique in scope. With this design, we can incorporate another database, PRICES, if our needs warrant it. We can also make the minor modifications necessary to include a LOCATION field if needed.

Note that we created part of our system much earlier. The part we just created will no doubt be used again and again with few or no modifications. Our calling system, however, may have modifications because the logic flow may be unique to a given environment.

The fact that we can use modules over and over leads us to our next subject.

Building a Library of Modules

Appendixes D through G show the templates DATABASE ACCESS MODULE, LABEL/ENVELOPE MAKER, WORDSTAR MAILMERGE MODULE, and "WHERE SENT" MODULE, which are used to track manuscript markets. Appendix H shows how all these modules can be linked.

You'll notice that the files in Appendixes D through G share many subroutines. They do so by DOing the subroutines, passing a parameter or two, or accessing the subroutines through a PROCEDURE file. Originally, all the subroutines were complete programs in themselves. But at some point the light came on, and I realized that I had no need for all those duplicate files on disk. The only differences were in the FRAMER, GETTER, DBF, and NDX file names, so I started building a library.

Library files are not new to high-level languages or dBASE III. Many languages (BASIC and MASM, for example) have runtime libraries, which are referenced during running, compilation, or both. This fact, along with the logic of dBASE III, provides a strong argument for the implementation of library files in dBASE III.

Essentially, your building blocks should be linked by function. For instance, you could partition a disk along logical lines like those found in the following TREE listing:

```
DIRECTORY PATH LISTING FOR VOLUME DBASE3BOOK

Path: \OTHER
Subdirectories: none

Path: \DBACCESS
Subdirectories: none

Path: \ACCOUNTI
Subdirectories: GL
                AP
                AR
                INVENTOR
                PAYROLL
                GJ

Path: \ACCOUNTI\GL
Subdirectories: none

Path: \ACCOUNTI\AP
Subdirectories: none


Path: \ACCOUNTI\AR
Subdirectories: none

Path: \ACCOUNTI\INVENTOR
Subdirectories: none

Path: \ACCOUNTI\PAYROLL
Subdirectories: none
```

```
Path: \ACCOUNTI\GJ
Subdirectories: none

Path: \MAILFUNC
Subdirectories: none

Path: \123TODB3
Subdirectories: none

Path: \MPLN2DB3
Subdirectories: none
```

Each directory contains separate modules with functions common to all the general dBASE III projects. I can modify and use the modules needed for each project. For a service-oriented business, more modifications may be necessary to the MAILFUNC modules than to others. Some businesses that already use Lotus 1-2-3 or Multiplan may need a little juggling of those modules without needing even to touch the ACCOUNTING modules. A merchandise-oriented business needs inventory control.

The MPLN2DB3 module was designed to provide a one-way bridge for getting a client's Multiplan files into dBASE III format. Later, another client needed a two-way bridge. The changes were easy enough to install and the modules have been used many times since.

Keeping the routines separate on disk facilitates linking them for different applications. Because each routine is complete, I don't have to worry about making fancy arrangements to use any one on a particular project. I determine which routines I need, make whatever (usually minor) adjustments are necessary for a project, determine whether the routines should be PROCEDUREized, and I'm done. If a new routine is developed, it goes in the library, with external documentation describing its function, purpose, original environment, and so on. Often I name the linked PROCEDURE files a library designate, such as ACCOUNT.LIB, recognizing the fact that dBASE III defaults to but is not limited to the PRG extension. Thus, my files often contain lines like

```
SET PROC TO ACCOUNT.LIB
SET PROC TO GL.LIB
SET PROC TO MAILLIST.LIB
SET PROC TO 123TODB3.LIB
```

and so on. These files execute with no problem.

I emphasize tasks, rather than jobs; modular coding; and writing tight, efficient code because I enjoy work but am not a workaholic. Readers with a background in mathematics will appreciate the following story, and recognize its truth in the previous discussion.

An engineer walks into a room and sees a fire in a corner and a bucket of sand close by. The engineer dumps the bucket of sand on the fire and puts it out, then leaves the room. A physicist walks into a room and sees a fire in a corner and a bucket of sand close by. The physicist pours a ring of sand around the fire, sits down, and observes the fire. A mathematician walks into a room and sees a fire in a corner and a bucket of sand close by. The mathematician realizes the problem can be solved and walks out of the room.

Advanced programmers don't like to work any harder than they have to. We're all mathematicians at heart.

5
Knowing dBASE III's Strengths

Because you're reading this book, I assume you have purchased dBASE III or are considering its purchase. Perhaps you purchased dBASE III because you have database work to do and you feel like going with the first and foremost, even though you don't know too much about the program. By now you do know that dBASE III is a logical language and an applications-development language. Now comes the time to investigate the strengths of dBASE III.

Inherent in the preceding statement is an acknowledgment of dBASE III's weaknesses. One of its principal weaknesses—at least according to many detractors—is "slow" execution. I should point out, however, that I do not feel that dBASE III is slower than the competition. If you put any two products side by side, you'll generally find that they do many things the same and some things differently. Hence, the "slowness" has never concerned me. I've learned to code around whatever slowness I feel exists. Much of this chapter is concerned with decreasing execution time.

My explorations in dBASE III have revealed a multitude of strengths, and I'm sure I haven't uncovered all of them. (I would be interested if any readers are willing to share their discoveries.) This chapter deals with those strengths, first on a theoretical level (the design of databases and index files) and then on a practical level (how using or not using certain commands affects the behavior of dBASE III).

Databases with Key Fields and Related Fields

Does database size and structure affect dBASE III's performance? Program I/O takes a great deal of time, but if the code is tight and to the point, program I/O usually occurs only once. The time needed for data I/O, however, is horrendous.

We can choose from several techniques for controlling and minimizing the time required for data I/O. Two techniques have been mentioned earlier: using an electronic disk or changing the number of available buffers.

But what if neither method is satisfactory? You design the database so that important information can be easily and quickly read. You can minimize data I/O by recognizing how dBASE III looks at databases. The key to minimizing data I/O is INDEXed files. The INDEXing is important, but it is not as crucial as designing the database so as to maximize the benefits provided by INDEXing.

When you are designing a database, especially one that is going to be INDEXed and REINDEXed fairly often, you should follow two rules:

1. Key fields go at the top of the database.
2. Related fields should be grouped together.

The following STUDENTS database applies these rules.

```
Structure for database   : C:STUDENTS.DBF
Number of data records   : 2
Date of last update      : 04/12/85

Field  Field name      Type         Width  Dec
  1    SNAME           Character      30
  2    SADDRESS        Character      30
  3    SCITY           Character      30
  4    SSTATE          Character       2
  5    SZIP            Character      10
  6    SPHONE          Character      10
```

7	MAJOR	Character	10
8	MINOR	Character	10
9	CLASSOF	Numeric	2
10	CLUB1	Character	10
11	CLUB2	Character	10
12	SPORT1	Character	10
13	SPORT2	Character	10
14	ASSOC1	Character	10
15	ASSOC2	Character	10
16	HONOR1	Character	10
17	HONOR2	Character	10
18	PNAME	Character	30
19	PADDRESS	Character	30
20	PCITY	Character	30
21	PSTATE	Character	2
22	PZIP	Character	10
23	PPHONE	Character	10
** Total **			327

In this database, student information is kept in one block; next comes alumni information, then parent information.

What makes this data structure efficient? Primarily, the structure is efficient because it follows the two rules I've stated. dBASE does not have to look through several fields to find indexkey; INDEXing is faster. Related blocks of data, such as the information needed when the Class of '85 leaves the school, can be COPYed, REPLACEd, or UPDATEd in one operation: dBASE doesn't have to get fields from positions 1, 5, 14, 15, 22, 30, and so on. When databases exceed a quarter megabyte of space, such niceties are appreciated.

How do you design a database this way? Two things come to mind; both have to do with forethought. First, you must recognize one characteristic of most clients: they are "sure" that every record needs 200 fields. Perhaps that is true for one or two functions of the program, but it certainly is not true for all functions. About 90 percent of day-to-day business operations do not use all the data the customers want in their databases. You must know when all the data is necessary and when only selected portions are necessary; then code accordingly.

Second, both dBASE III and dBASE II have a feature with which you can combine into one field what might otherwise take several fields. This feature can decrease database size.

Consider a partial database that keeps track of auto insurance policies. The insurance company keeps track of auto policies with information on MAKE, MODEL, YEAR, and VID. Our structure for the database is

```
Structure for database   :  C:AUTOPLCY.DBF
Number of data records   :  1000
Date of last update      :  05/28/85

Field  Field name    Type        Width   Dec
  1    MAKE          Character      3
  2    MODEL         Character      5
  3    YEAR          Character      2
  4    VID           Character     13
  .
  .
  .
```

Following these are several fields of less interest.

This structure is worthy, but it produces a large database. The insurance agency has told us that this information is looked at once or twice and after that is needed only rarely. The data is neither INDEXed nor SORTed on, but it is nonetheless important when you win the bet and your car is stolen.

A solution follows:

```
Structure for database   :  C:autoplcy.dbf
Number of data records   :  1000
Date of last update      :  05/28/85

Field  Field name    Type        Width   Dec
22     AUTO_INFO     Character     36
```

When this field is filled at data entry, we can use the following command line:

```
@ x,y SAY "Auto Information" GET AUTO_INFO;
PICTURE "mk!!! mdl!!!!! yrXX vid!!!!!!!!!!!!!"
```

We have decreased the size of our database on several fronts. First, the header block of the database has to keep track of three fewer fields. The database itself has three fewer fields to be scanned when looking for other information. The data is always accessible and now is stored in one line that actually makes more sense—to insurance people—than before. Finally, note that I moved the data down to a less important position in the database (field 22).

The Blank Record, or When Nothing Is Something

I have a subtle, little technique that has impressed clients to no end. The technique is simple to use, does not take up tons of room on disk or in memory, can be used on SORTed and INDEXed files with no difficulty, and makes your input, edit, and work screens look jazzy. The best use of the technique has been in applications where someone other than the keypunch operator has to use the database.

What is the technique? Simply place a blank record in your database. The record doesn't have to be totally blank; blank numeric database fields always contain zeros until you fill the fields. Most important is that the key field or fields you INDEX on must be blank.

To insert the blank record, you take an INDEXed database and APPEND BLANK. Then you never fill that one blank. Instead, you put new data in other APPENDed BLANKs. The INDEXed file automatically pops that blank record to the top of the file. When you first open (USE) the INDEXed database and DO some FRAMER and GETTER files, you immediately come to a clean, handsome screen. A screen like the one shown in figure 5.1 is much more pleasing than an unhighlighted (SET INTENSITY OFF) screen or a screenful of information that could be confusing, or at least distracting.

```
-V I E W                                                Today is -> 09/09/85

Name:        ANOTHER TEST NAME FOR A MAGAZINE
Address1:    AND A TEST ADDRESS
Address2:
City:                                 State:          Zip:
Country:                              Phone:

Contact:                              Dear:
Position:
Audience:                             Mss Length:

Qry: F    Mss: F    Sms: F    Dmp: ?    Gdi: F    Source:

Comment?: F                  Comment: memo


B(ack), D(isplay), F(ind), G(oto), L(ocate), C(ontinue), S(kip)      *
->
```

Fig. 5.1. A data-entry screen.

This simple technique, when used with any kind of custom data display, adds a highly professional touch.

Hiding Pictures in Databases

Now that you understand why a blank record can be a useful part of a database, I'm going to tell you the other side of the story. Sometimes, the format of an input screen needs to be changed in accordance with the value in a field or a memory variable.

An example can be seen in the insurance industry. Each type of insurance policy—preferred auto, standard homeowner, electronics and data processing, tenant, homeowner, and so on—has associated risk, coverage, and underwriter information. The nature of that information is different for each type of policy.

The following database shows an application of this principle.

```
Record#  INDEXFIELD FIELD1               FIELD2               FIELD3
    221  format-1   mkAAA  yr99          lien no xxxxxxxxxxxx lienholder AAAAAAAAA
    222  format-2   oldcode  XXXXXXX     newcode  XXXXXXXX    password XXXXXXXX
    223  format-3   carrier AAAAAAAAAAAA codetype XXXXXXXXXXX frequency 9999 AAAAA
```

Fields FIELD1, FIELD2, and FIELD3 are each twenty characters long. None of those fields holds information about individuals or items; instead, they hold pictures for screen formats 1, 2, and 3.

Before you learn how to use these pictures, consider where I have chosen to hide them. They are not in a memory file or in a database containing various picture formats. Instead, the pictures are in a database containing data—the data that is gathered through the input screens in which those pictures are used.

How are the pictures used? The following code demonstrates the elegance and simplicity of this method.

```
USE database INDEX indexfile
FINDER="format-"+var          ** var is the alpha code 1, 2, or 3
FIND &FINDER
F1=FIELD1                     ** F1 now holds the FIELD1 picture
F2=FIELD2                     ** for the corresponding alpha code;
F3=FIELD3                     ** ditto for F2 and F3.
APPEND BLANK
@ 10,0 GET FIELD1 PICT "&F1"  ** And now F1, F2, and F3 become the
@ 12,0 GET FIELD2 PICT "&F2"  ** PICTUREs for data input.
@ 14,0 GET FIELD3 PICT "&F3"
```

Masterbases and Smaller Databases

Unless a database is sorted along the lines of our search, the PC spends a lot of time filling buffers with useless information every time we search. Even then, all the information in each record of the database probably isn't needed for every database operation. Forty fields on the screen may seem impressive, but in reality the screen is busy and confusing, and the search is time-consuming to code and generate.

One of the easiest ways around this problem is to pull all required records from our masterbase into a smaller database. This method is useful, however, only if we can make certain assumptions about our necessary data:

1. The total number of records of necessary data should be significantly smaller than the entire master database.
2. The structure of the necessary database should be small compared to the structure of the entire database. Small is ten or fewer fields. (More on setting up databases later.)
3. The changes to be made should be different for each record.

This technique may take time at the outset, but we benefit because we then work with a smaller database file and operations on the data are more time-efficient.

Suppose, for example, that we want to enter new addresses for all 1985 graduates of Whatsamatta U. Out of more than 5,000 students, only 150 managed to graduate; we need to change only those 150 addresses. Our database is called STUDENTS. The database is INDEXed on SNAME, the SNAME field is 30 characters wide, and names are entered according to the following pattern:

LASTNAME,
FIRSTNAME, MIDDLE NAME OR INITIAL

The database has the following structure:

```
Structure for database    : C:students.dbf
Number of data records    : 2
Date of last update       : 01/01/80

Field  Field name    Type        Width   Dec
  1    SNAME         Character     30
  2    SADDRESS      Character     30
```

3	SCITY	Character	30
4	SSTATE	Character	2
5	SZIP	Character	10
6	SPHONE	Character	10
7	MAJOR	Character	10
8	MINOR	Character	10
9	CLASSOF	Numeric	2
10	CLUB1	Character	10
11	CLUB2	Character	10
12	SPORT1	Character	10
13	SPORT2	Character	10
14	ASSOC1	Character	10
15	ASSOC2	Character	10
16	HONOR1	Character	
17	HONOR2	Character	10
18	PNAME	Character	30
19	PADDRESS	Character	30
20	PCITY	Character	30
21	PSTATE	Character	2
22	PZIP	Character	10
23	PPHONE	Character	10
** Total **			327

We want to make changes to the records of all students in the class of '85. The following code does the job.

```
***UPDATER.PRG
USE STUDENTS
COPY TO GRADUATE FIELD SNAME, SADDRESS, SCITY, SSTATE, SZIP, SPHONE;
        FOR CLASSOF=YEAR(DATE())
SELECT 2
USE GRADUATE
INDEX ON SNAME TO GRADUATE
@ 20,0 SAY "CTRL-W to save and continue"
*
DO WHILE .NOT. EOF()
   EDIT
   SKIP
ENDDO
*
```

```
SELECT 1
USE STUDENTS INDEX SNAME
UPDATE ON SNAME FROM GRADUATE;
        REPLACE SADDRESS WITH GRADUATE->SADDRESS,;
        SCITY WITH GRADUATE->SCITY, SSTATE WITH GRADUATE->SSTATE,;
        SZIP WITH GRADUATE->SZIP, SPHONE WITH GRADUATE->SPHONE
CLOSE DATABASES
ERASE GRADUATE.DBF
ERASE GRADUATE.NDX
```

This method would make no sense if the same changes were made to every set; the REPLACE command would be easier to use in that case. But if the assumptions listed above are valid, we can use buffers quite nicely with this method.

First, we create a temporary database file called GRADUATE, into which we copy all the necessary records (everyone who is CLASSOF '85). We INDEX that temporary file on the student's name to make the file contiguous on a given field. This new database is contiguous in that it contains the records we're interested in: we've taken the separate CLASSOF '85 students and made a new database contiguous on that field. We make our changes and copy our edited data base back to our master file. The necessary data is small enough to be kept in buffers, and very little, if any, I/O occurs.

The question comes up as to whether UPDATER.PRG embodies the best method. That I can't answer. I can offer an alternate approach, however. This code uses one of the strengths of dBASE III and is listed as NEWUPDTR.PRG (see the section, "SET UNIQUE OFF/on, FOR, WHILE, and the Small NDX File" in Chapter 7). Differences between UPDATER.PRG and NEWUPDTR.PRG are shaded in NEWUPDTR.PRG.

NEWUPDTR.PRG keeps two databases active and works exclusively with INDEXed files. The STUDENTS databases is INDEXed on CLASSOF. NEWUPDTR.PRG first FINDs an entry that meets the criterion (the first CLASSOF '85 entry in the database) then COPYs WHILE that criterion is met. Changes are made to the new database in the same way, but data is written back to the original database according to an NDX in the NEWUPDTR.PRG. All in all, the two methods are valid. With larger subsets, I would choose the NEWUPDTR.PRG file.

The technique is to pull the necessary information from a much larger database and put it in a smaller temporary database. Work is done to the data in the smaller database. We create a smaller database that contains what we want, make our changes, then UPDATE the main database. This method makes for efficient data structures, as mentioned earlier.

We can use two or more temporary databases that pull information from a larger database. The only time the entire database in the Whatsamatta U. example is referenced is when records are added and edited. Every other operation references a subset of the fields used. In truth, STUDENTS.DBF is not large enough to warrant this method, but the example holds. This method temporarily decreases the number of files available in memory while minimizing the data I/O execution time.

An extension of this method is to have on disk two or more databases that have similar fields and share information. In many cases, data entry and editing need be done to only one of the databases; the others can be UPDATEd, APPENDed, or REPLACEd from the first. As always, an example follows.

The managers of a local video store want to keep track of VHS, Beta, and disk rentals. The managers also want a comprehensive list giving for each movie the supplier (with all related data), the store's catalog number, rental frequency, other suppliers, date received, and other data that won't really help in this example.

Obviously, the data has two distinct functions. One is keeping in-house records of orders; the other is compiling information on customers. Both functions use the store's catalog number. Data is entered only once—to the larger database at the time of initial data entry. All necessary information can be APPENDed to the second database after the new information has been entered.

In the example, the permanent databases are ALLINFO and SOMEINFO. ALLINFO is INDEXed on CAT_NUMBER. Similar fields in the two databases have identical field names. A third database, TEMPINFO, is used simply as a temporary storage vehicle.

```
USE ALLINFO INDEX INFO
COPY STRUC TO TEMPINFO
USE TEMPINFO

     [DATA IS ENTERED TO TEMPINFO]

APPEND FROM TEMPINFO
USE SOMEINFO
APPEND FROM TEMPINFO
```

Then, when the SOMEINFO database needs to be used, we can

```
USE SOMEINFO INDEX INFO
```

This presents no difficulties whatsoever, provided the value of the keyfield is never changed. We have created an NDX file that operates equally well on two (or more) databases, thus giving quick access. The true beauty of this method is that only one NDX file is opened. This factor cuts I/O significantly.

This method works because of dBASE III's NDX file structure. NDX files contain two relevant pieces of information about their related DBF files: keyfield value and record number. A simple representation is

Keyfield Value	*Record Number*
Andover	1
Boston	3
Hanover	10
Hanover	32
Kingston	4
Kingston	16
Kingston	100
Manchester	5
Melrose	6
Melrose	7

We are using primary and secondary keys in a database system (see Chapter 3). As long as the associated databases are APPENDed in the same order (as is done in the preceding code) and they share a keyfield, one NDX file serves all.

The Database Template

A strong argument can be made for the other side of a masterbase: the database template. The template concept shows its worth when data is going to be gathered and flushed, either for shipment of the database to another site or through ZAPping or PACKing, both of which are permanently destructive operations.

Let's assume that we have a central office receiving information from remote branches. Eventually, the central office decides to create one masterbase from all the different database files received.

Because all the information is to be APPENDed to one masterbase, all of the databases must have the same structure. The central office does not want to keep supplying the branches with clean databases for their work. Instead, at the time of setup, the central office gives each branch location a template. The database contains no records, only structure. When the branch office runs the system, the program first checks to see whether an active database is available. If not, the program creates an active database, as follows:

```
IF .NOT. FILE("database")
     USE template
     COPY TO database
ENDIF
**
USE database
```

Notice that we don't have to COPY STRUCTURE TO database in the preceding code segment. Because the template contains no records, we do not need to specify that we want only STRUCTURE.

Another value of the database template is in preserving database integrity. Working on our master database is not in the best interests of life. Please take the following rule to heart, engrave it in stone, tattoo it on your mate, whatever, but do remember it. It is JDI's Standard Rule of Programming #1.

Open an important file and

- lightning will strike.
- an earthquake will come.
- the dam will burst.
- you will be called to eternal rest.
- the dog will pull the cord out when you get up to get coffee.
- you will win the lottery and kick the cord out while pouring coffee on the motherboard.

Because I guarantee these things will happen, I am going to suggest another use of database templates, as demonstrated by the following code:

```
SELE A
USE database INDEX indexfile  *** THIS DATABASE HAS RECORDS IN IT
FIND var
COPY NEXT 1 TO template
SELE B
USE template
```

```
[MAKE ANY NECESSARY CHANGEs, EDITs, ETC.,]

SELE A
REPLACE FIELD1 WITH B->FIELD1, FIELD2 WITH B->FIELD2,...
```

If several records in the database are to be modified, the code can be changed so that REPLACEing doesn't occur at the end of each modification.

```
SELE A
USE database INDEX aindex
COPY STRUC TO template
SELE B
USE template
INDEX ON keyfield TO bindex        ***KEYFIELDS TO A AND B ARE THE SAME
ACCEPT "Find -> " TO var
DO WHILE TRIM(var)<>" "
   SELE A
   FIND var
   SELE B
   REPLACE NEXT 1 FIELD1 WITH A->FIELD1, FIELD2 WITH A->FIELD2,...

[MAKE MODIFICATIONS, EDITs, etc., TO THE TEMPLATE]

   ACCEPT "Find -> " TO var
ENDDO
**
DO WHILE .NOT. EOF()
   SELE A
   SEEK B->KEYFIELD
   REPLACE NEXT 1 FIELD1 WITH B->FIELD1, FIELD2 WITH B->FIELD2,...
   SELE B
   SKIP
ENDDO
```

The third and last use of the database template that I'm going to mention is also based on JDI's rule of the open database. This use has to do with adding new records to the database.

Don't open (USE) your master database simply to add records. In Appendix D, I demonstrate how to create a template to add new records. Your master database is opened (USEd) only twice during the entire operation: when the template is created and when the new records are APPENDed.

```
USE database
COPY STRUC TO template
USE template

[ADD RECORDS]

USE DATABASE
APPEND FROM template
```

Please note that, in this discussion and the rest of the book, I usually don't have many databases open at the same time. My reasoning is that the more databases I keep active, the more chance I have for a major kibosh. Just because a database is not currently selected doesn't mean the database is safe from damage should the inevitable happen. Hence JDI's Standard Rule of Programming #2:

> There are only two types of computer users:
>
> > Those who have experienced a major disk failure
> > Those who are going to experience a major disk failure

Index Files and Bell Curves

I have mentioned the fact that most data access is not random but follows certain curves (see Chapter 3). These curves give useful information for our clients in their business and for us in our coding. Consider our video store example. Is a curve possible for our primary index, the CAT_NUMBER? We note that our CAT_NUMBER is built on the following criteria:

1. First letter of store location
2. Type of medium (Beta or VHS)
3. First letters of first three significant words in title
4. Number of title in inventory of all titles (remember that each store has a list of all titles in all stores)

From CAT_NUMBER alone, therefore, we can get bell curves that reveal significant information for management. The records for the store that has the most titles in-house (first letter in CAT_NUMBER) can be compared with the total number of titles rented per day, week, or month. Note that, when the database is INDEXed on CAT_NUMBER, all titles from one store will be grouped together. If we find that we have two thousand titles in our Lebanon store, but only thirty titles were rented from that store, we know that the store is serving as little more than a warehouse. The second letter in CAT_NUMBER can tell what percentage of the titles are of what medium (VHS, Beta, disk). This figure tells management the best medium for the market and how to order.

Other bell curves can be made from the other fields in the database. What movies go out most often? Which go out least often? Where are most of our customers from? Do more people buy during promotions or not?

Without exception, you will find that the frequency of data access follows a bell curve on several fields. Usually, your client also knows (or at least suspects) this fact. You can ask about curves and ask to see graphs, if any are available, because they will be helpful in constructing programs. The standard bell curve in our example is shown in figure 5.2.

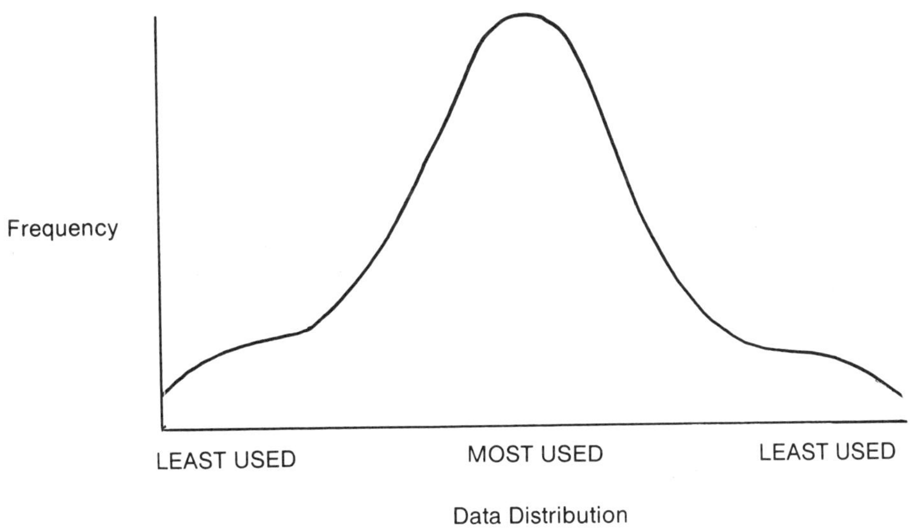

Fig. 5.2. The standard bell curve.

This curve helps us program in two ways. The curve can be used for data entry. The information from the bell curve helps us put the most frequently called functions at the beginning of our front end in a DO CASE . . . ENDCASE command.

The curve also helps us when we INDEX and LOCATE. Let's assume the curve tells us that most of our media are VHS. We want all titles in inventory that are VHS format.

```
SET EXACT OFF
SET PRINT ON
USE MOVIES INDEX INFO
FIND "LV"
LIST MOVIENAME, " Lebanon Store ", MOVIENAME, CAT_NUM WHILE CAT_NUM="LV"
FIND "HV"
LIST MOVIENAME, " Hanover Store ", MOVIENAME, CAT_NUM WHILE CAT_NUM="HV"
FIND "NV"
LIST MOVIENAME, " Norwich Store ", MOVIENAME, CAT_NUM WHILE CAT_NUM="NV"
SET PRINT OFF
```

This code gives us a quick-and-dirty list of requested titles. The list is not especially pretty, but it is a list, nonetheless. Pretty lists are produced by dBASE III's REPORT writer.

The point I'm making is that the LISTing recognizes that bell curves exist. The Lebanon store may have many titles, but we already know that we have more VHS titles than any other. What we do is FIND the first L(ebanon) V(HS) title, then LIST all the following titles WHILE they are VHS format. This operation is repeated for our Hanover and Norwich titles. The magic is that we've used an "ordered" random search; many would code a sequential search, as follows:

```
SET PRINT ON
USE MOVIES
LIST MOVIENAME, " Lebanon Store ", MOVIENAME, CAT_NUM WHILE CAT_NUM="LV"
LIST MOVIENAME, " Hanover Store ", MOVIENAME, CAT_NUM WHILE CAT_NUM="HV"
LIST MOVIENAME, " Norwich Store ", MOVIENAME, CAT_NUM WHILE CAT_NUM="NV"
SET PRINT OFF
```

Operations with Index Files

Several ways of using dBASE III's NDX files can make or break a system. Usually, the larger the environment, the larger the program system. The larger the system, the more databases are used. More databases usually mean more NDX files; hence, a knowledge of how dBASE III treats NDX files is vital to the programmer. This section deals with several aspects of NDX files and their use.

Using Primary and Secondary Keys

The video rental store provides an example of efficient use of primary and secondary keys in a database system. Let's say a customer wants to rent "The Never-Ending Story" for a VHS VCR. If we know that the information for "The Never-Ending Story" is in record 392, we can get the information simply by entering

```
GOTO 392
```

Unfortunately, we don't know the record number for each of the 5,000 titles in our inventory. What we do know is that "The Never-Ending Story" catalog number is LVNES?????.

That number has an easily remembered syntax, as explained previously. L(ebanon store) V(HS format) N(ever-)E(nding) S(tory), followed by a five-digit code that signifies that the movie is number such-and-such of so many movies in stock.

We don't know the five-digit code, a fact that makes sense because the customer doesn't care that the movie is number 3,019 of the 5,000 movies on our shelves. All we care about, when the customer is right there with money in hand, is whether the Lebanon store has "The Never-Ending Story" in the requested format. We may have five copies of "The Never-Ending Story" in VHS format at the Lebanon store. This method finds them for us:

```
SET EXACT OFF
USE SOMEINFO INDEX INFO
FIND "LVNES"
```

We are using a secondary key to reference the primary key (see Chapter 3).

Indexing on Concatenated Fields

I want to point out at the start of this discussion that I do not normally INDEX on concatenated fields. I try to keep keyfields between five and eight characters wide. That amount is normally enough to keep records separate.

One exception that comes to mind is a genealogy study conducted by a New York City group. The database consisted of the names of approximately 8,000 relatives spread all over the United States and Canada. (The family was both prolific and migratory.) From the start, it was obvious that we would have a tremendous duplicity of names. To INDEX using a standard LASTNAME+FIRSTNAME concatenation would have been ridiculous. Several hundred relatives with identical names lived in both New York City and Toronto, for instance, so using CITY was also unsatisfactory.

The solution was the bizarre concoction,

```
LASTNAME+FIRSTNAME+ZIPCODE+SUBSTR(PHONE,6,4)
```

This key worked well enough, except in FINDing and SEEKing; no one polling the database could correctly fit all the keys in an indexkey.

Moral: If you must INDEX on concatenated fields, try this kludge:

1. Determine the field lengths of the INDEXing fields:

```
Structure for database    : C:test.dbf
Number of data records    : 1
Date of last update       : 01/01/80

Field  Field name   Type        Width   Dec
  1    FIELD1       Character     10
  2    FIELD2       Character     13
  3    FIELD3       Character      6
  4    FIELD4       Character      8
  5    FIELD5       Character     20

  ** Total **                     58
```

2. Adjust the following template as necessary to get a workable value for FINDing or SEEKing:

```
STORE SPACE(20) TO F1,F2,F3,F4,F5
     @ 2,0 SAY "FIELD 1 -> " GET F1
     @ 3,0 SAY "FIELD 2 -> " GET F2
     @ 4,0 SAY "FIELD 3 -> " GET F3
     @ 5,0 SAY "FIELD 4 -> " GET F4
     @ 6,0 SAY "FIELD 5 -> " GET F5
     READ
     F1=TRIM(F1)
     F2=TRIM(F2)
     F3=TRIM(F3)
     F4=TRIM(F4)
     F5=TRIM(F5)
     FINDER=TRIM(F1-SPACE(10-LEN(F1))+F2-SPACE(13-LEN(F2))+F3-SPACE(6-LEN(F3));
            +F4-SPACE(8-LEN(F4))+F5-SPACE(20-LEN(F5)))
     SET EXACT OFF
     FIND &FINDER
```

The only note worth making is that I use TRIM, SPACE, and SET EXACT OFF to build and use the variable. This simple technique has proved invaluable.

Truncating Keyfields

In the previous section, I told how to FIND and SEEK using concatenated fields. In that discussion I said that the best keyfields are five to eight characters long. Now I explain my reasoning.

Let's consider several kinds of lists. Pick up your local telephone directory. Turn to any page and scan the names. With the possible exceptions of Adamses, Smiths, Joneses, and St. Somebodies, few names show similarities much beyond the eighth character. Those who live in a metropolitan area may find this experiment more profitable using phone numbers or addresses instead of names. Within area codes, no seven-digit phone numbers are repeated. (This is also a good example of knowing your data before you design the database.) Insurance records are keyed on a seven-digit code based on the last and first names of their clients. Account numbers range from four to seven digits. All in all, a keyfield of five to eight characters is normally safe. Naturally, this brevity improves the INDEXing speed when an INDEX or REINDEX is necessary.

Appending from the Start

If you've used the dBASE II or III INDEX command at all, you know that you can both APPEND and INSERT an INDEXed database. The new records show up where they should in the file. Pursuing this logic a step further, we can INDEX an empty database and APPEND and INSERT forever after. This method produces ordered random data from the first record entered.

A good idea is always to start a database with an NDX file, even if the client says an index is not needed. Nine times out of ten the need will arise. Good judgment in choosing a keyfield can save a lot of time farther down the road.

Creating Descending Indexes

The dBASE III manual claims that indexkeys can be done only in ascending order. I disagree. Getting a descending INDEX on a numeric database field is easy. You merely enter

```
INDEX ON -(numeric fieldname) TO indexfile
```

For instance, to generate an NDX file of checks paid from greatest amount to the least, you use

```
INDEX ON -AMOUNT TO indexfile
```

Doing this index with character database fields is a bit more difficult. The theory is the same, but remember that you have no such thing as a negative character. The trick is to use the ASC( ) function, as in

```
INDEX ON -ASC(character fieldname) TO indexfile
```

The preceding line INDEXes only on the first character in the string, but the pattern can be used as a guide for building more intricate character indexes in descending order. This technique, if used properly when the database is first designed, takes no more execution time than a normal indexkey.

COPYing an INDEXed File To Get a SORTed File

Now that I've explained how to get descending NDX files, I will explain why I developed the method. A particular client (a bulk-mail advertiser) required an application that performed a unique sort. The U.S. Postal Department likes things sorted by descending ZIP code. For bulk mailing, the ZIP codes are further broken down along other lines.

The client's representatives explained the postal regulations and stated that their database already had over thirty thousand names. It has since grown. SORTing through that large a database was an overnight job each time mailings had to go out (once a month). Another complication was that their PC was bandaged to a unique printer that put labels directly on the catalogs.

The solution uses the previously described method to generate a complete descending NDX file. To produce the labels, the database is COPYed rather than SORTed, an operation that saves a lot of time. The labels are generated from the COPYed file.

Using Multiple NDX Files

With dBASE III you can use several (up to seven) NDX files with the command,

```
SET INDEX TO indexfile
```

However, this command is best used to bring already active NDX files to the front of the system.

A more economical way of activating NDX files is to name them in the same line that USEs the database.

```
USE databasefile INDE indexfile1, indexfile2,...
```

This method automatically brings the first named NDX file to the front of the system while keeping subsequently named NDX files active. APPENDing, INSERTing, EDITing, and READing of records automatically modifies all active NDX files. Should you wish to bring another of the listed NDX files to the front, you can use

```
SET INDEX TO indexfile3, indexfile1, indexfile2
```

That statement switches the hierarchy of the NDX files for the FIND and SEEK commands.

You should note the following warnings:

Be careful when EDITing on the keyfield because you can blow up the referenced NDX file.

Errors can result when you try to open more than seven NDX files. These errors can drop you out of a program.

Weeding Out Duplicate Records

In this section, I demonstrate two methods of doing the same thing. The first method uses the "Bigger Hammer" method of programming. This method requires a lot of computer time and not too much experience with dBASE; it can do the job overnight. The second method uses one of the strengths of dBASE III. This method solves the same problem with some clever programming and requires a little knowledge about how dBASE III works but not much else. Best of all, it can do the same job in less than an hour. This second method uses the SET UNIQUE OFF/on command.

Our example originated when a local historical society tried to make a single workable database. The long and the short of it is that they ended up with three different databases, identical in structure. Each database contained duplicates of records in one or both of the other databases. One database ran from A through Z, another ran from A through L, and the third ran from M through Z. Each record of the three databases held several fields. The problem was compounded by the fact that different keypunch operators had entered new information in each database, and no two operators had entered the same information in any one of the three databases.

Begins to sound like one of those old logic problems, doesn't it? The catcher's name was Smith, and he ate strawberries on Sunday. The shortstop shot the conductor. What color is your lunch? The problem gets worse.

One day someone who had never before touched the computer wanted to get involved. The resulting error ate one entire database. This one database, which everybody knew held up-to-date membership data, was some 3,000 records long.

Fortunately, the society had backups for all the files. The managers wanted to know whether they could use an easy one-line command to merge all the databases, find the duplicated records and delete them, and then sort the members by identification number into a new database.

Let's look at this problem one step at a time. Is there a one-line command that could do all that? No. However, everything they've asked for is possible.

Certain things have to be done no matter which method we use. Merging the databases poses no problem. This operation is straightforward and easily done. Likewise, sorting the merged database is not a big shake. You can use either program I've listed in this section to sort (read INDEX) on any field; the interest in this example is on the identification number field. The middle request—finding the duplicated records and deleting them—is the key.

The first solution recognizes that dBASE can LOCATE, FIND, and SEEK. This is the "Bigger Hammer" method. Both FIND and SEEK work only on an indexed database, however. Further, these commands always stop at the first occurrence of what they're looking for. You can DELETE a record after it's found, but unless you PACK the database after each DELETion, SEEK and FIND still stop at the first occurrence.

The smart people out there are leaning toward LOCATE. Good. LOCATE is the first method we investigate. The solution is offered along with an explanation, as follows.

```
SET TALK OFF
CLEAR
USE C:MEMBERS
IF FILE('C:TANK.DBF')
   ERASE C:TANK.DBF
ENDIF
COPY STRUCTURE TO C:TANK
USE C:TANK
**
```

```
APPEND FROM C:MEMBERS
APPEND FROM C:MEMBACK
APPEND FROM C:MEMBACKX
**
COUNT TO LAST
STORE 1 TO N
STORE Ø TO M
**
DO WHILE N <> LAST
   GOTO N
   IF ID_NUM = "-1"
     STORE N+1 TO N
     LOOP
   ENDIF
   STORE ID_NUM TO LOOKER
   SKIP
   LOCATE NEXT (N-RECNO()) FOR LOOKER = ID_NUM
**
   IF LOOKER = ID_NUM
      STORE M+1 TO M
      REPLACE ID_NUM WITH "-1"
      DELETE
   ENDIF
**
   DO WHILE .NOT. EOF()
      CONTINUE
      IF LOOKER = ID_NUM
         STORE M+1 TO M
         REPLACE ID_NUM WITH "-1"
         DELETE
      ENDIF
    ENDDO
**
    STORE N+1 TO N
ENDDO
**
PACK
SORT ON ID_NUM TO MEMBER
**
@ 2Ø,1Ø SAY "Tra-la, Tra-la. It is done."
RETURN
```

TANK is a name I use to define a storage area. In this case, I use TANK to store all the data in the three databases. Rarely does someone employ my system of logic. In case someone does, though, I include the first IF . . . ENDIF test. Those lines look to see whether anybody else uses a TANK and erase it if found.

We have already placed the largest of the three databases in USE. After making sure no other TANKs exist, we COPY the STRUCTURE of the MEMBERS database TO C:TANK. Once this is done, we can input data to TANK exactly as if we were working with the MEMBERS database.

We then proceed to gather all the records into the TANK database. This is done by APPENDing FROM the three other databases (MEMBERS, MEMBACK, and MEMBACKX).

The meat of the program is in the DO . . . ENDDO loops. We start with N = 1. The value LAST is somewhere around 3,000. While N < > LAST, the program is directed to GOTO record N. We use -1 as a marker to indicate a duplicate record.

We know the program has already looked through a record IF we find ID_NUM = "-1" (at least, I've never thought of that as an identification number). If the program has looked through that record, the system LOOPs back and does a GOTO for the next record.

But if dBASE III doesn't find ID_NUM = "-1", the program STOREs the ID_NUM in LOOKER, which is just a variable name. Then the program SKIPs to the next record. RECNO( ) is the dBASE III function that tells us the number of the record being examined. The command

```
LOCATE NEXT (N-RECNO()) FOR LOOKER = ID_NUM
```

tells dBASE to look from where it is to the end of the database for duplications.

IF LOOKER = ID_NUM, dBASE III has found a duplicate record. The program marks that record for deletion by REPLACEing the ID_NUM with -1 and DELETEing it. Simply DELETEing the record won't do the trick unless we PACK the database at the same time. The "-1" gimmick is a nice bit of fudging that does the job.

Not all duplications are nearby in the database. The

```
DO WHILE .NOT. EOF()
```

ensures a perusal of the entire database by CONTINUEing the search until the program encounters the end of file. Eventually, I complete my search for duplications. The deletions are going to be permanent once I PACK the database.

I hope my explanation has proved informative. The operation is a nice exercise that gives you a feel for LOCATE, DO . . . ENDDO, and IF . . . ENDIF programming structures. That method is not what I really want to show you in this section, however; I have given that method only to show you what some forethought can do. Now I show you a better way.

The following program meets the same needs as the first program. This program, however, does the job much more quickly, much more neatly, and exhibits what we call *panache*.

```
SET UNIQUE ON
SET TALK OFF
CLEAR
USE C:MEMBERS
IF FILE('C:TANK.DBF')
   ERASE C:TANK.DBF
ENDIF
COPY STRUCTURE TO C:TANK
*
USE C:TANK
*
APPEND FROM C:MEMBERS
APPEND FROM C:MEMBACK
APPEND FROM C:MEMBACKX
*
INDEX ON ID_NUM TO NEWTANK
COPY TO MEMBER
@ 20,10 SAY "Tra-la, Tra-la. It is done."
RETURN
```

What makes this second method so clever? Well, we use the fact that dBASE itself can keep track of duplications in a file and weed them out. We use that capability in the first line of the second program,

```
SET UNIQUE ON
```

From there we proceed much as we did in the first program until we have APPENDed the three databases.

With the second program, I don't care about the amount of work because dBASE does the work for me. To delete duplicate files, I INDEX on the field of interest, ID_NUM, to an index file

(NEWTANK). The historical society wants a database called MEMBER. Fine, we COPY TO MEMBER. The program is clever—but even more clever, to those paying close attention, is that we got the sorted database without SORTing.

Operations with Memory Variables

Memory variables are what their name implies: variables that have nowhere to go but the memory of the machine. Memory variables are unlike database fields, which take up space in the database and in files and buffers. The problem is that memory variables are always active until dBASE leaves the routine using them or CLEARs them from memory with the RELEASE ALL or CLEAR MEMORY command.

The question therefore becomes: What can we do to achieve more efficient use of memory and memory variables? dBASE III provides many ways of using memory variables. Unfortunately, most of these ways are overlooked by most programmers.

The CONFIG.DB MVARSIZ Function

One dBASE III command can be used only when you are starting the dBASE III work session. In truth, the command isn't really a dBASE III command or function but a parameter that dBASE III uses to set up the computer. The command takes the form

```
MVARSIZ= n
```

where *n* can be any integer between 1 and 31.

The preceding command line can be placed anywhere in the CONFIG.DB file. The command tells dBASE III how much machine memory to use for memory variables. You say you've read "the book," and it says dBASE III has only 6,000 bytes for memory variable storage? Try this experiment. Use a word processor to enter in your present CONFIG.DB file the line

```
MVARSIZ=1
```

If your CONFIG.DB file already contains an MVARSIZ line, just write the line down somewhere. You can always put it back later.

Now start dBASE III and type

```
DISP MEMO
```

Because you've just started dBASE, no memory variables should be present. Even if memory variables are present, you should still see the following information on your screen:

```
  0 variables defined,          0 bytes used
256 variables available,     1024 bytes available
```

Now quit dBASE III and use your word processor to overwrite the old MVARSIZ line with

```
MVARSIZ=31
```

Start dBASE III again and DISPLAY the MEMORY. This time you'll see the message

```
  0 variables defined,          0 bytes used
256 variables available,    31744 bytes available
```

As you can see, changing the value of the MVARSIZ line in the CONFIG.DB file has dramatic affects on the memory management of the dBASE III system.

"So," you say, "even though I have increased the size of memory available for memory variables, I still have only 256 variables. What have I gained?"

You have gained precision. You still have 256 variables, but the precision of the values can extend to several decimal places when the MVARSIZ is high. Programmers who work with double-precision real values can appreciate this feature and will, I hope, make good use of it. This capability is a great advantage in engineering and scientific applications.

Three-Dimensional Arrays Using Memory Variables

Now that we know the true limit on memory variables is 256 variables total—not 6,000 bytes of storage—we can investigate ways to raise that 256-variable ceiling.

One method I use frequently is to create three-dimensional arrays. This construct is valuable because dBASE III itself doesn't directly support matrix operations. Using three-dimensional arrays makes array and matrix work (as found in both linear algebra and linear programming) much easier. I preface this discussion, however, by saying that this method involves some pretty fancy footwork but can be a real energy saver to programmers.

First, we have to agree on what an array is. Consider an illustration of a normal database:

```
          FIELD1    FIELD2    FIELD3    FIELD4    .....

RECORD1   R1F1      R1F2      R1F3      R1F4      .....

RECORD2   R2F1      R2F2      R2F3      R2F4      .....

RECORD3   R3F1      R3F2      R3F3      R3F4      .....

RECORD4   R4F1      R4F2      R4F3      R4F4      .....
   .
   .      ...       ...       ...       ...       ...
   .
```

If you're wondering what a spreadsheet is doing in a dBASE III book, then congratulate yourself. The diagram is a spreadsheet. A normal database is also a two-dimensional array, just like a spreadsheet.

Consider the everyday dBASE II or dBASE III database. It holds a collection of records; each record is a collection of fields. The records are numbered from 1 to whatever by dBASE III itself; the numbers then are used as primary keys. The fields are usually given names such as NAME, MAKE, YEAR, CODE, COST, and so on.

The illustration shows numbered fields. Let's assume that the field numbers correspond to field names as follows:

FIELD1 = NAME
FIELD2 = MAKE
FIELD3 = YEAR
FIELD4 = CODE
FIELD5 = COST

If we want to see the COST and MAKE of the car in record 4, we look in cells R4F5 and R4F2, respectively.

Now we go to three-dimensional arrays. Look at the illustration in figure 5.3. Those of you who studied physics or engineering will recognize that little plot, and you'll groan. But the plot serves as the focus and beginning block for this discussion.

The diagram is nothing more than a three-dimensional coordinate system with x, y, and z axes. This system is nothing to be afraid of. Just recognize that instead of being located by an (x,y) coordinate

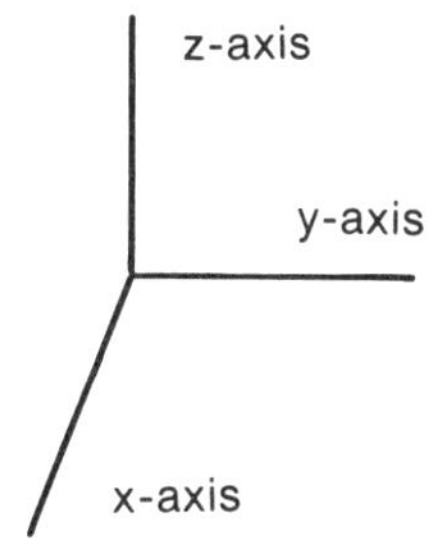

Fig. 5.3. Axes of a three-dimensional array.

pair, elements are located by an (x,y,z) coordinate triplet. People who have flown an airplane are familiar with three-dimensional arrays, even if they don't know it. If you are 30 miles north of Boston, 20 miles east of Boston, and 2 miles above Boston, you can say your location is (20,30,2) with reference to Boston.

Now we introduce a database, MEMFILES; fields in the database, MFILENAMES; and the memory variables themselves, running from MEMVAR1 to MEMVAR256 (see fig. 5.4).

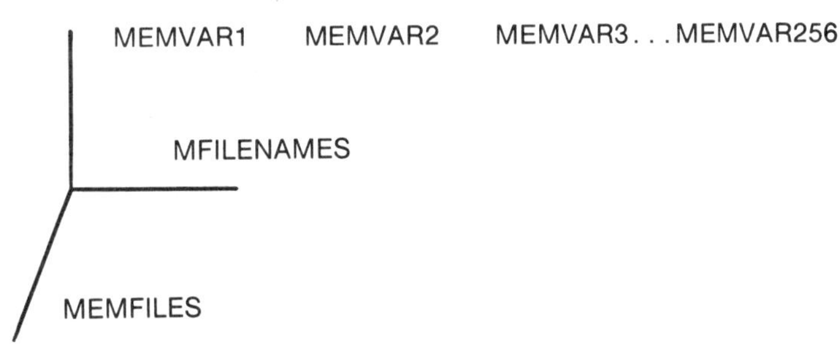

Fig. 5.4. Memory variables in a three-dimensional array.

Let's take a minute to analyze this construct. It is a true three-dimensional array. How so? Let's assume we have 256 memory-variable names available. We want a particular set of values for those variables, say for a certain cylinder rotation (as in a graphing operation) or for a coordinate translation such as changing the x,y,z triplet into a [ρ], [Θ], [Φ] triplet.

We USE the MEMFILES database, which is INDEXed on MFILENAMES, and

```
FIND/ep"XYZ2RTP"
```

This value in the MFILENAMES field is the key to the MEM file containing necessary values for translation from the XYZ system to the [ρ], [Θ], [Φ] system.

The other fields in this database record contain the names of the memory variables that handle the different translations from x,y,z to [ρ], [Θ], [Φ]. This record also contains the names of the variables that handle translations in the other direction. Because 256 variables are available to memory and 128 fields are available to each database record, one record can handle a large number of translations.

What does this capability gain you? Efficiency when many memory variables are active or are being juggled and changed throughout your work session.

You probably won't remember the names of all the variables, their values (which may change), or the names of the various MEM files you'll create and SAVE throughout the life of your program. But recognize that you have created a database template for the input of variables and values. Once this information is entered, your program can work with the information, eventually asking if the calculated values are to be saved for future use. If so, they can be placed in a MEM file. With this method, you can predefine MEM files, variables, and the like, to anticipate most manipulations simply by recognizing that no matter how varied the data, it will fit a certain template all the time. Through clever programming, you can even create your own variable names and MEM files by APPENDing the MEMFILES database and then READing responses to a standard entry screen.

This method has been used successfully, and some even have said it looks like artificial intelligence. That is a generous comment, albeit naive. The only intelligence in this method is on the part of the programmer, and precious little is artificial about that.

Memory Variables with Similar Names

Often, several variables on the same program level are very similar in intent. Because they are at the same level, the PUBLIC and PRIVATE commands are disabled. Giving each variable a different name adds to the confusion. The solution is to give each variable a similar, yet unique, name.

Once again, you may feel that your author has gone off the deep end. No, I haven't.

Consider an example with variables representing several cylinder sizes: CSIZE1, CSIZE2, CSIZE3, . . . CSIZE256, and perhaps even more. Cylinder size 2 is based on cylinder size 1; cylinder size 10 is based on cylinder sizes 1 through 9. This progression is typically called a *historical progression.* We don't want to create 256 or more variables and keep them floating in memory, but we do need to keep the cylinder sizes unique as they are created. In particular, we want each CSIZE variable to keep its own history, so that the variable name of the fourth cylinder size tells us that the size is derived from the sizes of cylinders 1, 2, and 3.

The solution makes use of dBASE III's MACRO function. We can't keep overwriting the CSIZE variable every time a new cylinder is created—that would wipe out the historical information—so we use the following trick:

```
CSIZE = "CSIZE4"
CHIST = "123"
NEWC = "&CSIZE.&CHIST"
```

The important trick is the inclusion of the period (.) in the last line of the example. The result is

```
NEWC = CSIZE4123
```

Using this trick, we can create several variables, all with similar yet unique names. These variables carry their history with them. Excellent for debugging, if nothing else.

Databases of Memory Variables

I have already described a method of creating three-dimensional arrays by using MEM files and databases. A similar method is to use databases as storage tanks for memory variables.

dBASE III MEM files are useful constructs, but crude and indelicate ones. A MEM file is loaded once and bypasses the buffers, which are a strength of the PC. One way around this problem is to create a database file to hold our memory variables. With this method, we can add selected memory variables to the program.

The central problem with MEM files is that you can retrieve them only with the RESTORE and RESTORE ADDITIVE commands. The former command destroys any existing values; the latter can create more than the maximum 256 memory variables, thus forcing dBASE III to argue vehemently with you in the middle of an application.

Use of a database to hold memory variables yields the following advantages:

1. Quicker access to the variables
2. Repeated access to values even if the related memory variable's value has changed
3. Use of buffers
4. The capability of selectively "restoring" memory variables without overwriting existing variable values
5. Better memory management because you can "restore" variables as they are needed, not all at once

Database Fields and Memory Variables with the Same Names

I've told you to make more use of database files when you are using memory variables. Now I'm going to show you how to use the same names for database fields and memory variables and still avoid confusion.

With dBASE III, you can keep up to ten databases active at one time. Correct? Actually, you have eleven. The eleventh "database" is the memory of the machine, where your memory variables are stored.

With dBASE III, you can reference the separate databases with

```
SELE A
SELE B
SELE C
```

and so on. You can reference the fields in the separate databases with

```
? A->FIELD1
? B->FIELD1
? C->FIELD1
```

and so on.

Now let's assume you have in USE a database with the field names COST, AMOUNT, and DISCOUNT. You also have memory variables named COST, AMOUNT, and DISCOUNT. dBASE II would get confused in some situations; dBASE III won't, if you remember the following facts:

1. Without a modifier (the A->, B->, and C->), the database field value is returned for any query to a particular name.
2. Database modifiers are A, B, C, through J.
3. The memory variable modifier is M.

Number three is the most important. The use of M-> is as follows:

```
->use testdbf

->disp struc

Structure for database  : C:TESTDBF.DBF
Number of data records  :       2
Date of last update     :   03/18/85
Field  Field name  Type         Width    Dec
    1  FIELD1      Character       10
    2  FIELD2      Character       10
    3  FIELD3      Numeric         10
** Total **                        31

->disp all

Record#  FIELD1     FIELD2          FIELD3
      1  hello      howdy               25
      2  goodbye    toodles              0

->1

->? field1

hello

->field1='yep, a change.'

yep, a change.

->? field1
```

```
hello

->? m->field1

yep, a change.
```

Notice that by including m-> we've separated the memory variable, field1, from the database field, also called field1. This is an important improvement over dBASE II and one worth exploring, if for no other reason than that it provides clarity in variable names.

You may have a database of client accounts with a field called BALANCE. At the end of the month you want to know the total due (the sum of the BALANCEs). You can't use TOTALDUE or SUMOFBAL because these names are used elsewhere in the same program and must be kept active. SAVEing them to a MEM file isn't worth the time. It is far easier to

```
SUM ON BALANCE TO BALANCE
```

and then reference the memory variable with M->BALANCE in subsequent parts of the program.

In this section, we've investigated methods of overcoming weaknesses by discovering strengths. Usually these strengths involve little more than some clever solutions to apparently difficult problems. I want you to remember what a "clever" solution is: something that's intuitively obvious after you've tried everything else and failed. Our clever solutions make use of little-known features of dBASE III in unique ways. Most of this book shows techniques that have been developed laboriously. But the point is simple enough: Wherever there is a weakness, there is a strength to overcome it.

6 Powerful but Overlooked Commands

Many dBASE III commands are poorly documented or rarely used, and wrongly so in both cases. These commands have been useful to my work, and a knowledge of them can be helpful to yours. So saying, I invite you to sample, experiment, and enjoy.

dBASE III's POKE and PEEK Commands

A command and a function that aren't documented in the dBASE III manual are POKE and PEEK. Many programmers, especially those familiar with BASIC, already know and use these commands. POKE and PEEK give experienced programmers considerable power over the machinery.

I'm not giving specific examples of the use of POKE or PEEK. Instead, I give general examples of how the two commands can be used and suggest that you get a copy of the technical reference manual for your particular PC or clone. The manual contains a list of memory locations that can be safely POKEd and PEEKed. The lack of specifics may be frustrating to novices and experts, but probably not to the vast realm of you who dwell in between.

I don't give specific examples because POKE and PEEK are not commands with which you can experiment haphazardly. Careful use can be a boon, but an improper listing can cause you to lose programs, data, files, the ability to exit from dBASE III when you want to, and even more frightening things. I give you what I feel is a "toe in the water," safe enough to let you know what is possible. I then leave the applications to you.

POKE and PEEK, respectively, manipulate and access specific memory locations in the computer. That capability can be very good or very bad. You can control output to peripherals without exiting to DOS; you can inadvertently write over the part of dBASE III that opens files or exits to the system. Ouch!

POKE is potentially the more damaging of the two commands because POKE actually alters memory values. The POKE command has the form

POKE memorylocation, value

Both memorylocation and value can be constants or computed values. POKE takes the numeric equivalent of value and puts that equivalent in memory at memorylocation.

PEEK is far less potentially damaging because PEEK just tells you what value is in a specific memorylocation. The PEEK command has the form

PEEK(memorylocation)

The memorylocation variable can be a constant or computed value. PEEK can be used in programs like any other dBASE III function.

The following listing is for a program called PEEKER. When we DO PEEKER, we see on the screen the decimal values of the contents of the first 1,000 bytes in machine memory. We take a PEEK at what's inside the machine's brain.

```
STORE 0 TO N
**
DO WHILE N<1000
 ? PEEK(N)
 STORE N+1 TO N
ENDDO
```

If you're an inexperienced programmer, take out your disks or back up your hard disk before experimenting. The POKE function can wreak havoc with disks. For those who wish to pursue the matter, the following are some of the more common manipulations that can be accomplished with POKE and PEEK:

1. Transfer output between printers or monitors without exiting to DOS or RUNning MODE
2. Test for the existence of peripheral equipment (for example, an active printer that may be in the next room and not turned on)
3. Determine available disk space before attempting to write a file
4. Alter the DOS method of error handling so that your program doesn't trash
5. Add sophisticated messages and audible warnings to your programs
6. Add your own password protection to dBASE applications
7. Set file parameters so that the file CAN'T/can be altered
8. Turn files into hidden system files.

(I find number 8 particularly useful when I suspect a client may welsh on a bill. I put a "worm" routine in the program; on the day of delivery, I set the routine to hide the files if I don't return in 32 days. If I'm paid on time I visit the site, saying I just want to make sure everything is running well and to provide an upgrade. If I don't come back, I haven't been paid; the client will call me, eventually.)

If you're not using POKE and PEEK already, this information should be enough to get you started. But be careful.

The Speed of SET CONSOLE ON/off

One dBASE III command gets much less use than it should; that command is SET CONSOLE ON/off. Normally, the CONSOLE is SET ON, and that setting is fine for 99% of the work dBASE III does. At times, however, we have no need for the screen to be on. DOing a program and monitoring the console also takes more time than just DOing a program.

We notice the greatest savings of time in programs that need little user input and hence don't have to keep the user informed as to what has been going on. This consideration leads us to another important one: the psychology of the user. Users like to know something is going on. When a machine appears dead, they likely will either kick it (reboot)—or they themselves will expire. Fortunately, the SET CONSOLE ON/off command gives some flexibility regarding both the user's and the machine's mortality.

This command doesn't alter what is already on the screen. SET CONSOLE ON/off merely prevents dBASE from checking to see whether each subsequent command has to send information to the console. The nature of the command means that we can write code like the following:

```
SET COLOR TO 5*
TEXT
   WW     WW   OOOOOOOO  RRRRRRRR  KK     KK  IIIIIII  NN      NN  GGGGGGGG
   WW     WW   OO    OO  RR     R  KK    KK      II    NNN     NN  GG     G
   WW     WW   OO    OO  RR     R  KK   KK       II    NN N    NN  GG
   WW  WW WW   OO    OO  RRRRRRRR  KKKK          II    NN  N   NN  GG   GGG
   WW  WW WW   OO    OO  RRRR      KK KK         II    NN   N  NN  GG     G
   WW  WW WW   OO    OO  RR  RR    KK    KK      II    NN     NNN  GG     G
   WWWWWWWWW   OOOOOOOO  RR    RR  KK     KK  IIIIIII  NN     NNN  GGGGGGGG
ENDTEXT
SET COLOR TO W, ,
?"                    !!PLEASE DO NOT DISTURB!!"
SET CONSOLE OFF

    [block of working code]

SET CONSOLE ON
```

This display ensures (we hope) that the computer is left to work uninterrupted; the code gives dBASE III the added speed that can be gained from not monitoring the console at each step in the program.

REPLACEing with Provisions

For those who aren't familiar with the REPLACE command, the basic syntax is

> REPLACE [range] fieldname(s) WITH value(s) [FOR/WHILE condition]

REPLACE is used to change the values in specific fields in the USEd database.

Experience has shown me that this command is not as widely used as it could be. The best use of the command, aside from REPLACEing values that have been entered incorrectly, and so forth, is for finishing the job of data entry. The example in this section has to do with a central office that gets disks of data from remote sites.

The object of the lesson is to speed entry and manipulation of data by requiring the keypunch personnel to enter only the data that changes in each entry, not data that is the same for record after record. This technique is obviously useful in that it speeds up data entry; it is also useful in that it minimizes errors in entry of repetitious data. Unless your keypunch personnel are vegetables, entry of repetitious data will cause their minds and hearts to wander to golden beaches or snowcapped peaks—anywhere but the CRT.

I have often used the concepts of masterbase and database in this book. Now I turn to the other side of the balance: the database template. The logic for the database template is explained here.

Let's go back to the example of a central office with branch offices reporting to it. The branches gather data about their areas, and the form of the data gathered is the same no matter what the location. The database file structure might be as follows:

```
Structure for database    :  C:REMOTES.DBF
Number of data records    :  0
Date of last update       :  12/30/84

Field  Field name         Type        Width   Dec
  1    NAME               Character     30
  2    DEAR               Character     15
  3    HADDRESS           Character     30
  4    BADDRESS           Character     30
  5    PHONE              Character      8
  6    CITY               Character     20
  7    STATE              Character      2
  8    ZIP                Character      5
  9    AREACODE           Character      5

  ** Total **                          146
```

Each branch office has a DBACCESS module much like the one in Appendix D. The DBACCESS module handles the bulk of database functions. The separate parts allow for addition of records, DELETion of records, PACKing the database, viewing the database, EDITing records and similar functions. The FRAMER and GETTER modules produce a screen like the one shown in figure 6.1.

```
=====================================================================================
-!!                  !!                                                            !!
 !! This screen is   !!                                                            !!
 !! for use by the   !!  Name          ->    Ralph Richardson                      !!
 !! remote offices   !!  Home Address  ->    Up in the mountains                   !!
 !! to enter data    !!  Busi Address  ->    Down in the valley                    !!
 !!                  !!  Phone         ->    555-1212                              !!
 !!                  !!                                                            !!
 !!                  !!                                                            !!
-------------------------------------------------------------------------------------
 !!                  !!                                                            !!
 !! This screen is   !!  Name          ->    Ralph Richardson                      !!
 !! for use by the   !!  Home Address  ->    Up in the mountains                   !!
 !! central office   !!  Busi Address  ->    Down in the valley                    !!
 !! to examine and   !!  City          ->    Manchester                            !!
 !! edit collected   !!  State         ->    NH  Zip ->   03104                    !!
 !! data from the    !!  Phone         ->    (603) 555-1212                        !!
 !! remote stations. !!                                                            !!
=====================================================================================

->
```

Fig. 6.1. Data-entry screen for remote sales.

At some point, the disk must be shipped from the branch to the central office. On the main menu, put the following option:

```
F9 -> SHIP DISK
```

Make sure your client knows that this option doesn't RUN the DOS PARK or SHIPDISK program. Selection of that option causes the following block of code to run:

```
CASE response=247
   CLEAR
   SET COLO TO 5*
   @ 10,0 SAY SPACE(20)+"FIXING"
   REPLACE ALL CITY WITH cityname, STATE WITH stateid,;
               ZIP WITH zipcode, AREACODE WITH areacode
```

```
SET COLO TO 7*
@ 10,0 SAY SPACE(20)+"LOCKING"
[PERHAPS A POKE TO MAKE THE DATABASE UNALTERABLE]
SET COLO TO W, ,
CLEAR
@ 10,0 SAY SPACE(20)+"PLEASE REMOVE DISK"
```

This code provides a simple example of the REPLACE command. Stronger uses of the REPLACE command are shown in the sections entitled "Combinations Rarely Used" and "dBASE III's One-Line Loops."

STRING Operators in Place of LOGICAL Operators

Let's assume two conditions are given. The result of a test on those conditions is valid if either condition exists. The two conditions cannot coexist, so we don't worry about that possibility. What is the easiest and safest method for coding that comparison test? Most people would choose

```
IF "&var"="condition1" .OR. "&var"="condition2"
```

Right? Wrong!

A better way to code the comparison is with one of these equivalent statements:

```
IF AT('&var','condition1 condition2')<>0
```

or

```
IF '&var' $ 'condition1 condition2'
```

The space between *condition1* and *condition2* is intentional. It prevents true statements from occurring when the value of var equals an unintended combination of the conditions. An example would definitely help.

```
var='radar'
condition1='adar'
condition2='adar'
```

We want to know if the value of var is equal to either the value of condition1 or condition2, but not a combination of the values.

```
IF '&var' $ 'condition1 condition2'
```

becomes

```
IF 'radar' $ 'adar adar'
```

which is false. However,

```
IF '&var' $ 'condition1condition2'
```

becomes

```
If 'radar' $ 'adaradar'
```

which is logically true, but programmatically false.

The first example returns a value greater than zero if the var can be found in either condition. The second example returns a logical value of .T. if var can be found in condition1 condition2. It returns a logical .F. if var can't be found in condition1 condition2.

The most obvious use of this kind of test is in systems that ask the user to enter information for comparison to data in a database. The test is also used as a request for data from a database (see Appendixes D through H).

In this example, the test is used with string variables and operators. Similar tests can be used with numeric variables by first converting them to their STR equivalents.

Arithmetic on DATE Fields

Programmers can use the DATE( ) function, DATE variables, and their properties to add a certain degree of sophistication to programs. We can do arithmetic with DATE variables and fields, but the operations are limited: we are limited to adding and subtracting numbers to and from DATEs and subtracting one DATE from another.

Earlier in this chapter, I mentioned that this capability can be used to activate a "worm" routine. A more conventional yet still inventive use of these capabilities is to determine when databases should be created or closed. The typical example is a polling system. Most polling systems close out at regular specified intervals: 7 days, 30 days, 120 days, and so on. We don't have to rely on the operator to know when a particular polling database should be closed. We can let the program determine that time for us.

The following code assumes the existence of a system clock or some other reliable way of ascertaining the date.

```
starter=.T.
CLEAR
@ 10,10 "Does today start a new polling session (Y/N)? -> " GET STARTER
IF starter
   startdate=DATE()
   SAVE startdate TO BEGIN
ELSE
   REST FROM BEGIN
ENDIF
**
IF DATE()=startdate+pollperiod          ** POLLPERIOD IS THE
   USE database                         ** LENGTH OF THE POLL.
   COPY STRUC TO newdatabase            ** IT IS STORED IN THE
                                        ** BEGIN.MEM FILE
   [POSSIBLE COPYING OF STRUCTURE TO A NEW DISK, ETC.]
ENDIF

[WORKING BLOCK OF CODE]
```

Arithmetic operations on DATE variables also can be used to solve some typical accounting problems. We can test for past-due accounts simply by having a DUEDATE field in each record in our RECEIVABLES file and testing with

```
IF DATE()-DATEDUE<0
DO NOTICE2 WITH DATEDUE, BALANCE
```

Past-due accounts can then be flagged and messages can be sent.

Using DISPLAY and GOTO with SET RELATION TO

Many programmers hesitate to use dBASE III's work areas because they see the work areas as providing little more than do the SELECT PRIMARY and SELECT SECONDARY commands. In this section and the next, I present often overlooked ways of using several databases, referencing the concept of primary and secondary keys (see "Primary and Secondary Keys" in Chapter 3), which is relevant to this and the next section.

As I have mentioned, the computer uses a primary key to keep track of information, and the secondary key is how we mortals keep track of things. Let's imagine we have one masterbase, DBA, and several databases containing related information—DBB, DBC, DBD, and so on. All the related databases have information in common with DBA but not with each other. The exception is one keyfield that is also the indexfield for DBA (see fig. 6.2).

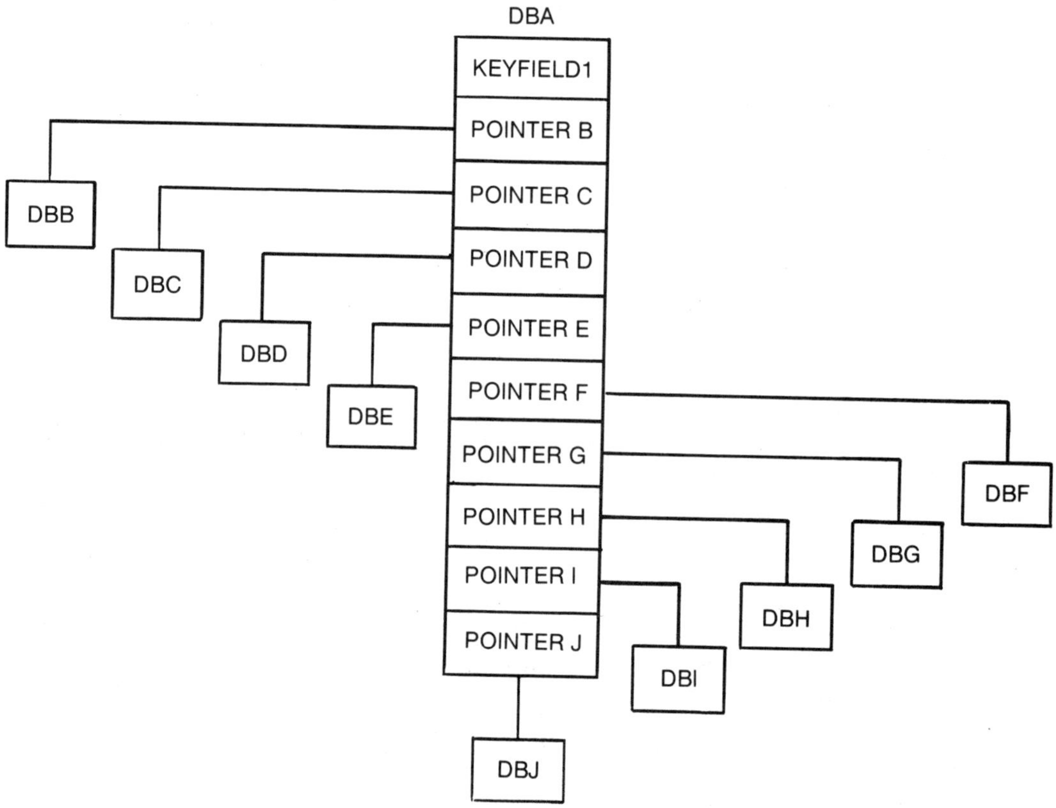

Fig. 6.2. A masterbase and related databases.

Only DBA is INDEXed. The fact to remember is that DBA is both *pointing to* and *being* pointed to by all the other databases because of the RELATION we set up. We open the files plainly enough with

```
USE DBA INDEX AINDEX
SELE B
USE DBB
SET RELATION TO AFIELD1 INTO A
SELE C
USE DBC
SET RELATION TO AFIELD1 INTO A
SELE D
USE DBD
SET RELATION TO AFIELD1 INTO A
```

and so on down to database DBG. Remember that AFIELD1 is the keyfield for database DBA.

We reference databases DBB through DBJ by using the fields of our pointer file. To DISPLAY the related information in DBG, we can

```
SELE A
FIND var
SELE G
GOTO RECNO() A
```

This code is an example of "pointing." We know the indexkey in database DBA. We want to find the related information in database DBG. We FIND the INDEXKEY in DBA, switch to DBG, and instruct dBASE III to GOTO the RECNO( ) pointed to by the database record in work area A.

The ability to point to one work area from another work area is a powerful construct; I strongly recommend that you experiment with it in your own applications. It can save many program steps.

As another method of making the other databases point to DBA, we can use

```
DISP A->AFIELD10, GFIELD10, GFIELD5,...
```

Again, to compare values or related fields in different databases, we can

```
SELE A
FIND var
SELE G
GOTO RECNO() A
SELE C
GOTO RECNO() A
SELE F
GOTO RECNO() A
DISP A->AFIELDx, G->GFIELDy, C->CFIELDz, F->FFIELDt
```

This is another powerful but overlooked construct in dBASE III. I advise you to experiment before using this construct in a program; you may have to make a few trial runs to achieve the desired result.

The Difference between SEEK and FIND

SEEK and FIND are the dBASE III commands used to quickly GOTO INDEXed records. Both commands are based on indexkeys and keyfields. First, we look at similarities, then at differences.

Assume you have a 2,000-record database of clients INDEXed on the NAME field. You've entered the names carefully, so each is unique. Now you want to find Jack Jickjock's name and pull his record. Using FIND, you could do either

```
FIND Jack Jickjock
```

or

```
STORE 'Jack Jickjock' to ANAME
FIND &ANAME
```

Using SEEK, you either

```
SEEK 'Jack Jickjock'
```

or

```
STORE 'Jack Jickjock' to ANAME
SEEK ANAME
```

As you can see, both commands do the same job, only differently. One of the problems with using SEEK instead of FIND results from a programming prejudice based on the dBASE III manual.

The dBASE III manual says that we cannot use macros within control structures. Actually, we are warned that using macros within control structures causes the program to execute more slowly and also may cause confusion. I believe the reference is to users being confused by a program listing.

The dBASE III control structures are DO WHILE . . . ENDDO (with or without EXIT or LOOP), DO CASE . . . ENDCASE (with or without OTHERWISE), and IF . . . ENDIF (with or without ELSE). The brave ones among you have already realized that you can use macros inside control structures without headache.

For many applications (obviously those where cross-referencing is vital), the SEEK command is the method of choice. It can be used in all applications (at least those I've tried) without restriction.

Using SEEK instead of FIND in a dBASE III control structure has an advantage in time of .002 seconds. Hardly significant. After 1,000 passes, FIND increases execution time by only 2 seconds. However, if you are a purist, this economy can be meaningful. If you're programming massive amounts of code, with repeated requests for information from an INDEXed database, the advantage may be worth having.

The reason for using SEEK when coding is that it makes less work for the computer. SEEK eliminates one manipulation: conversion of FIND &VAR into the proper form. That omission also eliminates one chance for making a mistake.

So much for using SEEK and FIND on the same database to find the same information. There is one more highly significant difference between FIND and SEEK. To demonstrate this difference, I again use the concept of database and masterbase. Assume that the database has 2,000 records with 10 fields. The masterbase has 2,000 records with 50 fields. The masterbase was INDEXed when we created it (even though there were no records to INDEX) with the keyfield MFIELD1. The database was also INDEXed from the first, so each APPENDing updated the index file accordingly. The database's keyfield is DFIELD1. DFIELD10 corresponds to MFIELD1.

```
USE database INDEX dindexfile
FIND var
SELE B
USE masterbase INDEX mindexfile
SEEK A->DFIELD10
```

To further demonstrate this powerful construct, let's assume we have seven active database-indexfile combinations. They are linked in a way similar to the method described in the previous section. This time, however, the fields in DBA contain the indexkeys for databases DBB through DBG.

Database DBA is INDEXed on field DBA-1, DBB on field DBB-1, and so on. Further,

DBA-2	corresponds to DBB-1
DBA-3	corresponds to DBC-1
DBA-4	corresponds to DBD-1
DBA-5	corresponds to DBE-1
DBA-6	corresponds to DBF-1
DBA-7	corresponds to DBG-1

Our primary database is DBA, which is also a powerful indexfile to databases DBB through DBG. If all seven database-indexfile combinations are active, we can use the following code:

```
USE DBA INDE AINDEX
SELE B
USE DBB INDE BINDEX
SELE C
USE DBC INDE CINDEX
SELE D
USE DBD INDE DINDEX
SELE E
USE DBE INDE EINDEX
SELE F
USE DBF INDE FINDEX
SELE G
USE DBG INDE GINDEX
```

We can pull up data in DBE, for example, when all we know is the related keyfield for DBA.

```
SELE A
FIND var
SELE E
SEEK A->DBA-5
```

Also note that any of the databases can be used to define the SEEK field for any of the other databases, provided the field being sought is the keyfield.

The RANGE Delimiter as an Error Check

Most dBASE II and III programmers have worked to death the limits of @ SAY . . . GET and @ SAY . . . GET PICTURE. One valuable option, however, is rarely used. The limits of data input can be predetermined through use of the RANGE delimiter, as in the following line:

```
@ SAY ... GET RANGE lowvalue, highvalue
```

This command works with all dBASE III variable types and can provide a useful on-line error check. By using the system date, we can provide a means of limiting the dates of entry with

```
@ x,y SAY "Date of transaction -> " GET transdate RANGE;
DATE()-100, DATE()+100
```

Another useful check is to ensure the proper range for data entry of numeric variables:

```
@ x,y SAY "Percentage rate -> " GET prate RANGE 0,100
```

You can use expressions, constants, or database field values as RANGE arguments. The RANGE command is also capable of accepting arguments from other active databases, such as

```
@ x,y SAY "New value -> " GET var RANGE A->AFIELD, B->BFIELD
```

The power of the RANGE delimiter is that it can take any valid dBASE III value or argument and use it as part of the error check. Accounting systems can check that entries are made between the start of the month and the system date, engineering systems can determine if valid temperature ranges are entered based on given scales of measurement, and so on.

7 Rare Combinations

Just as dBASE III has some powerful but overlooked commands, it also has several powerful but overlooked combinations. Some of these combinations simply add pizzazz to a data input screen; others can serve as useful error-checks or allow wider FIND and SEEK tolerances.

Cross-Referencing Other Databases

The dBASE III work areas and the COPY STRUCTURE EXTENDED command can provide a particularly clean error check. This check takes advantage of dBASE III's capability of evaluating expressions in one work area by comparing them to another.

Assume, for instance, that you have designed a system that checks immediate information against a larger body of past information. An example of this type of system is the check cashing machine that uses a "secret number" to make sure that you are who you claim to be. These devices check your given reference against a historic reference.

A similar system is feasible with dBASE III. The system can be used to check memberships, member status, affiliation, or any other information that can be referenced from one database to another. Such a system requires two databases: one to contain the master file information, and one to store the structure file of the first database. You create these databases with

```
USE adatabase
COPY STRUC EXTENDED TO bdatabase
```

The following code can then perform the error check:

```
USE adatabase INDEX IDS
ACCE "CODE-> " TO id
FIND &id
SELE B
USE bdatabase INDEX PWS
ACCE "PASSWORD -> " TO pw
FIND &pw
**
DO WHILE .NOT. EOF()
   IF id=A->&ID_NUM
      ? "ACCEPTED"
      EXIT
   ENDIF
   SKIP
ENDDO
```

We are using two separate databases. One of the databases, adatabase, contains ID numbers and other nonvolatile data. For the purposes of the above code, the other data isn't even referenced. An example in keeping with the magic money machine example concept would be setting the adatabase to count number of accesses in one day, amount of deposit or withdrawal per access, number of incorrect entry attempts and so on.

Once we find immediately necessary information in adatabase we get more information from bdatabase. Notice that each database checks the other's data. Each database is keyed on a different item, but their data overlaps for the purpose of validating entry.

Collapsing Databases with ZAP and PACK

DBASE III provides two commands whose function is, in essence, to collapse databases. One command is ZAP, and the other is PACK. You can use ZAP if you want to collapse all the records in your database quickly. If you use PACK on a large database, the process can be slow. You didn't buy your computer to slow down your work, so the moral here is "Don't PACK."

You will often want to back up an important database, even if you plan to delete some of the database records. Instead of PACKing, use the commands RENAME and COPY TO:

```
oldbase="&database"+".old"
RENAME &database TO &oldbase
SET DELETED ON
USE oldbase
COPY TO database
USE database
```

This routine is simple, clean, and neat. We've created a backup file and "packed" the work file in about the time required to PACK the database normally.

Creating Database Subsets by COPYing with a FILTER

The COPY TO command can also be used with the SET FILTER TO command. This combination, used in conjunction with the method described in the last section, can help you design some uniquely "packed" databases. This is a strong combination because you can SET FILTER TO anything: a value, a database field or fields, the database fields of other work areas, and so on.

The best use of this command is to create subset database files. Consider the video-store example of Chapter 5. If you want to create a database for the records of everyone in the Hanover area, you would

```
USE customers
SET FILTER TO CITY="Hanover"
COPY TO hanover
USE hanover
```

The syntax used to reference another work area's database field is the same as in the method presented earlier:

```
SELE D
SET FILT TO CITY=A->CITY
COPY TO acity
```

The SET FILTER TO command also allows for the use of multiple conditions:

```
SET FILT TO CITY="Hanover"+LASTNAME=A->LASTNAME+...
```

In this way, you can perform highly selective COPYs.

Note: The SET FILTER TO command requires logical operators, such as < > , = , + , and .NOT.

Performing Specialized Searches with SET UNIQUE OFF/ON

Imagine we need to send a mailing to a small subgroup of the people named in a database, and each of those persons' records has a common item in a common field. We can now see the power of the SET UNIQUE OFF/on command, and we'll combine that power with that of the FOR and WHILE qualifiers to produce some fancy searches.

SET UNIQUE ON was used in the historical society example to weed out duplicate records. Now we'll use SET UNIQUE ON to create an NDX file that is kept active with a large database. The database may have a thousand repetitive records. The important consideration is that the keyfield is somewhat repetitive throughout the database. The indexfile can have as few as twenty or thirty pointers, depending on how often the keyfield changes. The key is that the NDX file is not representative of the entire database; it is more like a series of road signs.

How do we use the NDX file as a series of road signs? First, we create the NDX file:

```
SET UNIQUE ON
USE database
INDEX ON KEYFIELD TO indexfile
```

At this point, the indexfile contains the road signs that are needed for the job at hand. We want to send letters to everyone whose record meets the condition

```
KEYFIELD=indexkey
```

All we need is this routine:

```
FIND "indexkey"
DO WHILE KEYFIELD="indexkey"
[WORKING CODE]
SKIP
ENDDO
```

Depending on how the records are to be pulled and where they are found in the database, we can substitute one or more of dBASE's one-line loops for the DO WHILE. . . ENDDO structure.

We can make the search even more specific by including a FOR qualifier. The WHILE qualifier ensures that only contiguous records with KEYFIELD="indexkey" are accepted. The WHILE qualifier is a logical tool; the FOR qualifier is a sequential tool. The FOR qualifier can select several special cases from the subgroup, as in this routine:

```
SET UNIQ ON
USE database
INDEX ON KEYFIELD TO indexfile
FIND "indexkey"
DO WHILE KEYFIELD="indexkey"

   [WORKING CODE] FOR FIELDx="var"  ** If a looping command is
                                    ** used, the syntax would be
   SKIP                             ** [WORKING CODE] NEXT 1 FOR;
ENDDO                               ** FIELDx="var"
```

An alternative to this method is, of course, to design the indexfile with more than one keyfield. That method would produce code like this:

```
SET UNIQ ON
USE database
INDEX ON KEYFIELD1+KEYFIELD2+ ...  TO indexfile
FIND "indexkey"
DO WHILE KEYFIELD1="(first part of indexkey)" .AND. KEYFIELD2=;
        "(second part of indexkey)" .AND.  ...

    [WORKING CODE]

    SKIP
ENDDO
```

The indexkey in the example must be the entire keyfield construct, unless the SET EXACT OFF option is used. This may not be what we want, however: dBASE will find the only best match, not necessarily the right match.

The problem of Whatsamatta U.'s Class of '85 provides a useful example. We can use SET UNIQUE and WHILE to make a quick-acting block of code, if we have used SET UNIQUE ON in creating the NDX file.

```
*** NEWUPDTR.PRG
USE STUDENTS INDEX GRADYEAR
FIND YEAR(DATE())
COPY TO GRADUATE FIELD SNAME, SADDRESS, SCITY, SSTATE, SZIP, SPHONE;
        WHILE CLASSOF=YEAR(DATE())
SELECT 2
USE GRADUATE
INDEX ON SNAME TO GRADUATE
@ 20,0 SAY "CTRL-W to save and continue"
*
DO WHILE .NOT. EOF()
  EDIT
  SKIP
ENDDO
*
SELECT 1
SET INDEX TO SNAME
UPDATE ON SNAME FROM GRADUATE;
        REPLACE SADDRESS WITH GRADUATE->SADDRESS, ;
        SCITY WITH GRADUATE->SCITY, SSTATE WITH GRADUATE->SSTATE, ;
        SZIP WITH GRADUATE->SZIP, SPHONE WITH GRADUATE->SPHONE
RUN ERASE GRADUATE
```

Remember that the GRADYEAR NDX file in line 1 was created using SET UNIQUE ON. The NDX file therefore only contains pointers to the first record found for each year. The STUDENTS database may contain several thousand records with CLASSOF field values from 66 to 90, but the NDX file will only contain twenty-five pointers: one for the first entry for CLASSOF=66, one for the first entry for CLASSOF=67, and so on. However, the DBF file is still organized so that all CLASSOF=66 entries are together, all CLASSOF=67 entries are together, and so on.

In line 2 we FIND the first record that meets our search criterion. The WHILE clause in line 3 can be used because all desired records are contiguous. We switch NDX files in line 15 merely to allow UPDATEing in the SNAME field, which is our field of primary interest and was our keyfield in the GRADUATE database. Line 17 is just a quick way of getting rid of temporary files.

What is the difference between NEWUPDTR.PRG and UPDATER.PRG? Because I have designed a similar system for a local college, I now know that the university plans to INDEX on more than one field for different updates. NEWUPDTR.PRG takes that knowledge into account.

The people at the university added memory to their machines, so I could RUN DOS, BASIC, and ASSEMBLER programs from dBASE III. Is this faster than UPDATER.PRG? I don't know. But the program did what the customer wanted, made the customer happy, and earned a paycheck for me. And those are the three things that count.

Performing Sophisticated Searches with a FILTERed INDEX

Take any large file with duplicated records—such as the genealogical study—and we can use the SET FILTER TO command to perform searches so highly defined that we can pick one desired record out of a crowd. Although this command doesn't alter the size of the index file, SET FILTER TO does change the size of the output.

We begin as in the last example, INDEXing with SET UNIQUE ON. However, the difference is the output.

```
SET UNIQUE ON
USE database
INDEX ON KEYFIELD TO indexfile
SET FILTER TO filter1, filter2,  ...
FIND "indexkey"
DO WHILE KEYFIELD="indexkey"

   [WORKING CODE]        ** This can include the 'FOR'
                         ** qualifier
ENDDO
```

You can use the SET FILTER TO command with the precision of a surgical blade to winnow out individuals or small groups. Remember, however, that SET FILTER TO is a *logical* construct.

Fancy Data Entry with SET DELIMITER TO and SET COLOR TO

I have often wondered about the psychology of data entry. I know that the task is, at best, tedious and boring. I didn't like to enter data. I performed this function for the Navy for several months, using IBM keypunch equipment. Even the development of the inexpensive CRT has not lessened the tediousness of the job. Data-entry people still tend to forget to enter all the data in all the fields, or at least to enter the important data in the fields of major interest.

These tendencies became a major problem when one of my clients needed an incredible volume of information entered to a database. Four keypunch operators worked eight hours a day for one month; such is the lot of the undergraduate work-study student. I needed to develop a method that would alert the operators when they had left something out. The solution was a combination of the SET DELIMITER TO, SET DELIMITER ON, and SET COLOR TO commands. This combination created a screen like the one shown in figure 7.1.

```
-V I E W                                          Today is ->  09/09/85

 Name:      >Que Corporation                          <
 Address1:  >7999 Knue Rd                             <
 Address2:  >Suite 202                                <
 City:      >Indianapolis            <State:   >IN<  Zip:  >46250    <
 Country:   >USA            <         Phone:   >(317) 555-1212<

 Contact:   >Pegg Kennedy            <Dear:    >Pegg              <
 Position:  >Acquisitions Editor <
 Audience:  >Computer junkies        <Mss Length:  >300 pages     <

 Qry:  >y<   Mss:  >y<   Sms:  >n<   Dmp:  >y<   Gdi:  >y<  Source:  >Pegg      <

 Comment?:  >y<                   Comment:  >memo<

 B(ack), D(isplay), F(ind), G(oto), L(ocate), C(ontinue), S(kip)     > <
->
```

Fig. 7.1. A data-entry screen.

Unfortunately, I can't show you the full impact of the screen in this book. I therefore suggest that you write some matched FRAMER and GETTER routines, like those in appendix H, then enter the following program.

```
SET DELIMITER TO "><" ** The delimiters can be anything you want.
SET DELIMITER ON
DO &framer
SET COLOR TO 5*          ** Determine which blinking color is the
DO &getter               ** most obnoxious for your monitor
SET COLOR TO W, ,        ** Set the color back to the standard
READ                     ** display
```

You can see the two-color effect when editing and adding data. The adding screen shows blinking delimiters; the colors change when you enter new data. The editing screen shows the old data, blinking in a horrid color. The fields stop blinking and change color as new data is entered. The result is quite effective.

FINDing Data with SET EXACT and AT

Many programmers use dBASE III's SET EXACT ON/off command to "unqualify" the FIND commands in their programs. The SET EXACT ON command instructs dBASE III to FIND only strings or values that match exactly. For example, you can FIND or SEEK an indexkey such as *Hel*, when the actual keyfield value is *Hello*. *Hello* equals *Hel* when SET EXACT is OFF.

This command is obviously useful when you are searching for information in an INDEXed database: you don't need to know the entire keyfield value to use an indexkey. Unfortunately, the SET EXACT ON/off only finds the first characters of a string. If a FIND or SEEK returns a NO FIND argument, you can use

```
LOCATE FOR AT(partial keyfield value, KEYFIELD)<>0
```

This method takes more time than does using a FIND or SEEK, but it can help you find records when you know only a part of the keyfield. You can make the code work faster by adding SET INDEX TO with no argument in order to close all index files.

REPORTing with the SET RELATION TO Command

REPORT used with SET RELATION TO is a useful combination. It allows you to CREATE or MODIFY REPORT forms so that they can use information from other databases. All you need to do is to specify the unselected database and its field in the FIELD CONTENTS section when CREATEing or MODIFYing the REPORT, as is shown in figure 7.2.

```
Structure of file C:MAGAZINE.dbf

NAME        C  50  |STATE      C   2  |DEAR        C  20  |PHONE      C  15
ADDRESS1    C  50  |COUNTRY    C  20  |POSITION    C  20  |GDL        L   1
ADDRESS2    C  50  |ZIP        C  10  |AUDIENCE    C  30  |QRY        L   1
CITY        C  30  |CONTACT    C  30  |MSSLENGTH   C  15  |DMP        L   1

                                       Field  1          Columns left =   41
>>>>>>>>CITY

          XXXXXXXXXXXXXXXXXXXXXXXXXXXXXX

Field       >A->CITY
  contents
                                                                          <
                                  # decimal places: >0<Total? (Y/N): >N

           1>CITY                                                          <
Field      2>                                                              <
  header   3>                                                              <
           4>                                                              <
Width      >30<
```

Fig. 7.2. Referencing an unselected database.

This combination, when used with SET RELATION TO, creates a powerful cross-referencing report generator. An example of its use is the creation of reports from an advertising agency's lists of media and clients. The client database includes a MARKET field, which stores information on the client's market audience. The media database has a TARGET field, which stores information on the target audience. The information is listed under different field names in the two databases, but it is the same information.

If we are REPORTing on the CLIENT database, we can use the following routine:

```
USE MEDIA INDEX TARGET
SELE B
USE CLIENT
SET RELA TO MARKET INTO MEDIA
REPORT FORM MARKETS
```

Depending on what REPORT FORM is used, this structure generates reports that match several fields from one database to fields in the related database.

In a similar example, you can use a MAGAZINE database with an AUDIENCE field and a MSS (manuscript) database to match manuscripts to magazines based on audience.

Figures 7.3 and 7.4 demonstrate how simple this combination is to execute. Figure 7.3 shows a FIELD CONTENTS description based on the field of interest in our primary use database. The same REPORT form can then access information from another, unselected database, as is shown in Figure 7.4. dBASE III permits only one RELATION per work area. However, ten RELATIONS can be in use at one time. This capability, with some clever database design, allows for several cross references.

Testing for Data Input with CASE and ASC

The CASE and ASC combination can be used to test for any type of data input. The effectiveness of the combination derives from the fact that the dBASE III CASE command checks for only one condition. That condition, however, can be defined by means of the =, <, and > operators. The condition can also incorporate any of the other arithmetic or logical tests.

We can use the CASE command with the ASC( ) function to determine whether a user's response is numeric, alphabetic, a control code, or a function key. Fortunately, the ASC( ) function is not particular about the argument it receives. ASC( ) simply returns the ASCII character code of the first character of the argument.

Assume that the user can press one of several characters to perform certain operations on the database: C for CHANGE, E for EDIT, or S for SKIP. In addition to these alphabetic inputs, the user can enter

```
Structure of file C:MSS.dbf

MSS_NAME    C  30
AUDIENCE    C  30
MSSLENGTH   C  10
FIRSTPARAG  M  10

                                     Field  1          Columns left =   72
>>>>>>>>------------------------------------------------------------------


Field        MSS_NAME
  contents

                          # decimal places: 0  Total? (Y/N): N

            1MANUSCRIPT
Field       2
  header    3
            4
Width       30
```

Fig. 7.3. FIELD CONTENTS description for the primary database.

numeric characters to call selected records from the same database or another; 1 and 2 would then have the following meanings:

1 for SELE 1, 2 for SELE 2

1 to put one database in USE, 2 to USE another database

1 for GOTO 1, 2 for GOTO 2, etc.

By using ASC( ) and CASE, we can test such options as follows:

```
***JDIMAIN.CMD FOR CENTURION CORP
***DESIGNED BY JOSEPH-DAVID CARRABIS, APRIL '85
**
CLEAR
SELE A
USE NEWINS INDE NEWINS
SELE B
USE NEWPLCY INDE NEWPLCY
DO NEWFRAME
```

```
Structure of file C:MSS.dbf

MSS_NAME    C  30  |            |            |
AUDIENCE    C  30  |            |            |
MSSLENGTH   C  10  |            |            |
FIRSTPARAG  M  10  |            |            |

                              Field  2          Columns left =    10
>>>>>>>>>MANUSCRIPT          MAGAZINE                    ----------


      XXXXXXXXXXXXXXXXXXXXXXXXXXXXXX XXXXXXXXXXXXXXXXXXXXXXXXXXXXXX

Field           MAGAZINE->NAME
  contents



                              # decimal places: 0  Total? (Y/N): N

               1MAGAZINE
Field          2
  header       3
               4
Width          30
```

Fig. 7.4. FIELD CONTENTS description for the second database.

```
**
DO WHIL .T.
   SELE A
   DO NEWGETS
   SELE B
   DO CPOLFRAM
   DO CPOLGETS
   CLEA GETS
   @ 21,Ø
   ACCE "(C)hange  (R)evise  (N)ext  (B)ack  (P)rint  (E)nd" to A
**
   DO CASE
      CASE ASC(A)<49
         @ 21,Ø
WAIT "Valid selections are 1-9,C,R,N,B,P, or E. Press any key to continue"
```

```
**
    CASE ASC(A)<58
       STORE RECNO() TO NEWINSREC
       STORE "P"+STR(A,1,Ø) TO P_FIELD
       STORE &P_FIELD TO POL_TYPE
       STORE REC TO FINDER
       DO JDIPLCY
       SELECT A
       USE NEWINS IDNE NEWINS
       SELECT B
       USE INS INDE INS
       CLEAR
       DO NEWFRAME
**
    CASE ASC(A)>57
       STORE UPPER(A) TO A
**
       DO CASE
          CASE A="C"
             @ 21,Ø CLEAR
             ACCE "What is the new client code? -> " TO CLI_CODE
             STORE UPPER(CLI_CODE) TO CLI_CODE
**
             IF CLI_CODE="NEW"
                DO MISC
             ELSE
                USE INS INDE INS
                FIND &CLI_CODE
                COPY NEXT 1 TO INSTANK
                SELE A
                APPEND FROM INSTANK
             ENDIF
**
          CASE A="R"
             DO NEWSOME
             DO CPOLGETS
             @ 21,Ø CLEAR
             @ 21,Ø SAY "Type Ctrl-W to exit"
             READ
**
          CASE A="N"
             SKIP
```

```
**
            CASE A="B"
               SKIP -1
**
            CASE A="P"
               SET DEVICE TO PRINT
               DO NEWINS.FMT
               SET DEVICE TO SCREEN
**
            CASE A="E"
               RETURN
**
            OTHE
               @ 21,0
 WAIT "Valid selections are 1-9,C,R,N,B,P, or E. Type any key to continue"
         ENDCASE
**
   ENDCASE
**
ENDDO
```

I created the first DO CASE . . . ENDCASE set to determine whether the variable A is alphabetic or numeric input. If A is alphabetic, the CASE statements pass execution to the second DO CASE . . . ENDCASE set.

8 Parameters and Public Variables

This chapter offers a theoretical discussion of the PUBLIC, PRIVATE, DO PARAMETERS, and RELEASE commands. Like the rest of this book, this chapter is meant to provide a foundation for you to build on. This chapter also offers a discussion of how these commands work.

The main point in this section is that a variable declared in a calling program can be used in a called program and returned to the calling program. The variable can return to the program changed in value, and—if you're not careful—changed in type.

Accessing PUBLIC Variables

DBASE III needs to "know" which variables are local to one program and which variables can move back and forth between programs. The simplest way to make a variable capable of moving back and forth is to declare the variable PUBLIC.

Declaring a variable PUBLIC is similar to using the COMMON command in BASIC. The dBASE III manual describes the command as *global*; some programmers may remember the term. The PRIVATE command is comparable to the LOCAL command of some other languages.

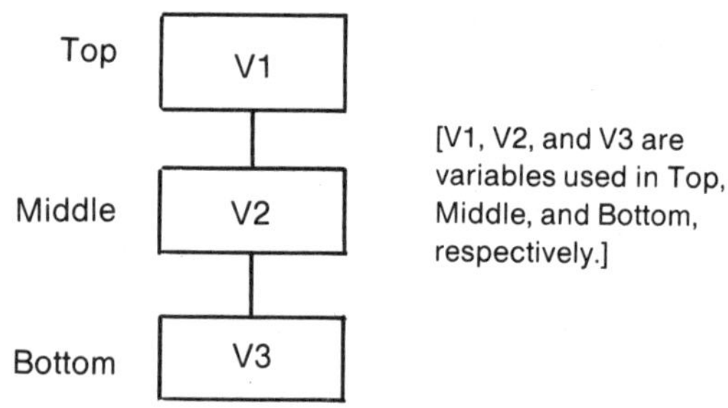

Fig. 8.1. A hierarchical program with variables at different levels.

Figure 8.1 shows a hierarchical program structure composed of three programs. Their names indicate their position in the hierarchy. TOP calls MIDDLE, which then calls BOTTOM, but TOP cannot directly call BOTTOM. Each of the memory variables, V1, V2, and V3, is declared in its respective program.

Assume that we want to pass some information among the programs; there's no point in linking programs that cannot pass data back and forth.

We'll begin with the simple case: passing information from TOP to BOTTOM. This case most closely resembles the method of dBASE II and requires no special commands. Once declared, all variables are accessible routines at all levels. You can always pass information down levels.

Variable V1 can be accessed by all three programs. Variable V2 can be accessed by the two lower programs. Variable V3 can only be accessed by the last program.

Read the last three sentences again. A message is hidden there.

The message is this: *What is accessed can be changed.* If BOTTOM makes changes to V1 or V2, the changes are transferred through the hierarchy. However, variables declared in lower-level programs are hidden from higher-level programs, because variables are LOCAL to the programs, subroutines, and procedures that call them. The TOP program therefore gives you an error message if you query about V2 or V3. The MIDDLE program gives you an error message if you query about V3.

All variables are automatically RELEASEd when program execution ends. RELEASE is a dBASE IIIism for *destroy*: memory variables declared in a program cannot be accessed after the declaring program ends. You therefore cannot access V2 after MIDDLE has ended, or V3 after BOTTOM has ended.

What if you want to use V2 and V3 in TOP? You can declare all three variables at the beginning of TOP, making them available to any program. That is the easiest way to give all three programs access to the variables.

If you want the variables to remain available after all three programs are terminated, you can declare the variables PUBLIC either before you DO any of the programs or at the beginning of TOP. For example, assume that you want V3 to remain after the TOP, MIDDLE, and BOTTOM programs have executed. Before you can access V3, you must include the command PUBLIC V3.

You will receive an error message if you make a variable PUBLIC after it has been declared. PUBLIC variables assume a LOGICAL value (.T. or .F.) until declared.

Accessing PRIVATE Variables

The opposite of the PUBLIC command is the PRIVATE command. Whereas the PUBLIC command makes a variable available to any level of the program, the PRIVATE command keeps a variable within a certain level. If V1 is declared in TOP, then ordinarily TOP, MIDDLE, and BOTTOM are able to manipulate the variable. But what if you want to use the variable name V1 in the MIDDLE program without using the value assigned to V1 in the TOP program? Then you use PRIVATE V1 in MIDDLE before you use the name V1.

Then you need to declare V1 again, or you will receive an error message. What is the hidden meaning this time?

To understand the answer to that question, assume that you enter the PRIVATE V1 command at the tenth line of the MIDDLE program, and that you worked with V1 before issuing that command. Figure 8.2 graphically illustrates that assumption.

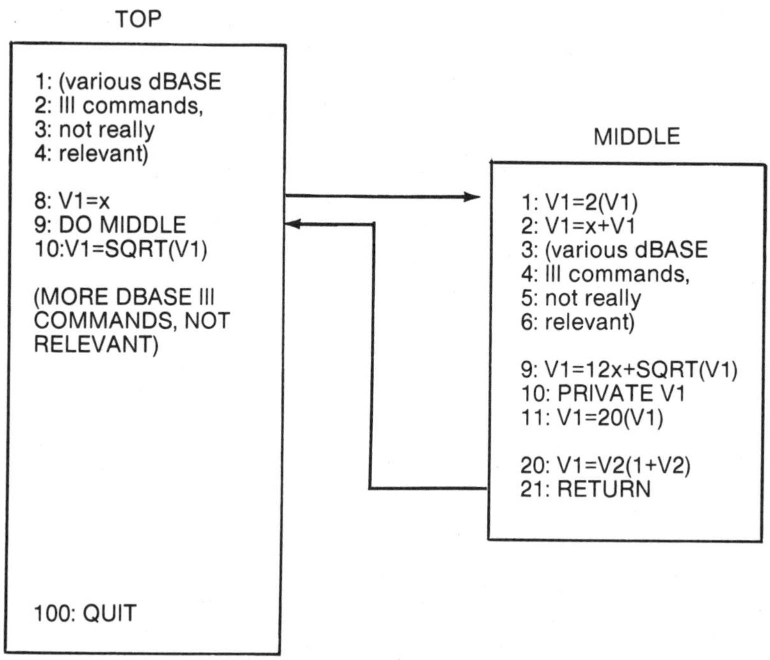

Fig. 8.2. Interaction of the programs TOP and MIDDLE.

The value returned to TOP at line 21 of MIDDLE is the value assigned in line 9 of MIDDLE. All manipulations done on V1 after it is declared PRIVATE in line 10 of MIDDLE are not RETURNed to TOP when MIDDLE finishes execution. However, the value of V1 RETURNed to TOP is not the same as the one passed to MIDDLE. Even though V1 is declared PRIVATE in line 10 of MIDDLE, all manipulations done on V1 prior to that declaration are RETURNed to the calling program, in this case TOP.

The other message is that making a variable PRIVATE only stops the value stored in the variable from flowing up, not down. If the BOTTOM program uses a variable named V1, the value of the variable is determined in MIDDLE, not in TOP.

You should never use more memory variables than necessary, because the variables tie up valuable memory space. After the program is executed, all PRIVATE variables are released. Periodically (especially if you have a large system), you need to "clean out" your memory with

```
RELEASE ALL LIKE variabletype
```

or

```
RELEASE variable1, variable2,...
```

dBASE III provides a bridge between PUBLIC and PRIVATE in the DO WITH . . . PARAMETERS command set. You can use these commands to send information to a subroutine "incognito." In this case, you want the subroutine to perform tasks with the value of a variable without using the variable name. You can do this easily.

Suppose you have a fourth program called OTHER that is not listed in the diagram of figure 8.1. With OTHER included, the diagram appears as in figure 8.3.

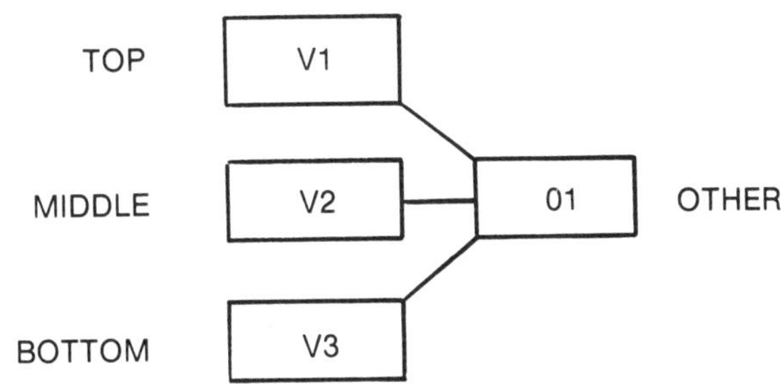

Fig. 8.3. A program passing data to a hierarachical program structure.

OTHER has the variable O1. OTHER manipulates data necessary to TOP, MIDDLE, and BOTTOM. You need to pass along to OTHER the value of V1, V2 and V3 without OTHER's using the variable names. You can DO OTHER WITH V1 (or V2 or V3, as the situation requires) to call OTHER.

The first command in OTHER must be PARAMETERS O1. No further declarations are necessary. Then OTHER can manipulate the value of V1 (or V2 or V3), as stored in O1, without actually affecting V1. All changes are made to the variable O1. This trick is useful when you want to compare a value (V1) with an anticipated value (O1) that is determined by performing calculations on V1.

The hidden message here is that the value of O1 is passed to V1 upon termination of OTHER. Even though V1 remains unchanged while OTHER is working, V1 takes the value of O1 when OTHER is terminated. Because of this fact, you must be careful.

One-Line Loops with dBASE III

A loop is a block of code that performs a task repeatedly. dBASE III has several commands that perform loops. An example of a one-line loop is

```
COUNT TO NUMBER
```

This simple one-line loop actually accomplishes the same result as the follow code sequence:

```
NUMBER=Ø
GOTO TOP
DO WHILE .NOT. EOF()
   NUMBER=NUMBER+1
   SKIP
ENDDO
```

In the same way, the one-line loop

```
TOTAL TO SUMMARY ON FIELD1,FIELD2...
```

performs the same function as the following lengthy block of code:

```
STORE Ø TO F1,F2,...
USE DATABASE
COPY STRUC TO SUMMARY
DO WHILE .NOT. EOF()
   F1=F1+FIELD1
   F2=F2+FIELD2
   .   .   .
   .   .   .
   .   .   .
   SKIP
ENDDO
USE SUMMARY
APPEND BLANK
REPLACE FIELD1 WITH F1,FIELD2 WITH F2,...
```

The last example of a one-line loop uses the SUM command. The one-line loop

```
SUM FIELD1,FIELD2... TO F1,F2...
```

replaces the entire code block

```
STORE Ø TO F1,F2,...
GOTO TOP
DO WHILE .NOT. EOF()
   F1=F1+FIELD1
   F2=F2+FIELD2
   .  .  .
   .  .  .
   .  .  .
   SKIP
ENDDO
```

If my point is obscure, I apologize. I want you to know that you don't need to reinvent the wheel. The one-line loops listed illustrate two points I want to make in this section:

1. Make the maximum use of minimum code
2. If a loop is necessary, keep it small

The point is to code your loops to perform only a specific function. If you code for any contingency, you will create a time-consuming and unwieldy loop. If you read my recoding of the one-line loops, you'll notice that the commands only contain the necessary instructions.

Using FOR and WHILE Qualifiers

Be especially careful when you use the FOR and WHILE qualifiers. When you use WHILE, you will see either the data you requested or nothing, depending on the setting of the database pointer. For example, assume that you want to REPORT something WHILE a condition is true. You use

```
REPORT FORM reportfile WHILE condition
```

If the database pointer is on a record where the condition is not true, no REPORT is generated, although there may be several other records in the database that meet the condition. To solve this problem, you can use a random one-line loop, such as

```
REPORT FORM reportfile FOR condition
```

This command starts from the database pointer location and proceeds until EOF() is True, checking every record for "condition"=.T.

You can also get around this problem by using a method listed earlier. Use an NDX file to FIND or SEEK the first occurrence of "condition." Once the first occurrence of "condition" has been found, you can use the WHILE qualifier to poll the selected records.

dBASE III commands which allow both FOR and WHILE qualifiers are

AVERAGE determines the mean value of any number of fields. These fields don't have to be in the SELECTED database. For example, look at the following code:

```
USE ADATABASE              ** Which has 200
                           records
SELE B USE BDATABASE       ** Which has 2000
                           records
SELE A
AVER B->BFIELD1
```

This program returns the mean value of the first two hundred entries in BFIELD1 in the database BDATABASE. Combinations of conditions based on the fields in work-area databases can be used. You can use AVERAGE to produce random samplings of a database based on the entries in another database.

CHANGE allows selective editing of a database WHILE or FOR a user-supplied condition. This command can be combined with SET RELATION TO to provide conditional CHANGEs based on two criteria: the user-supplied condition and the entries in a database in a non-SELECTED area.

COPY can be used with qualifiers on both the SELECTED and non-SELECTED database. For example,

```
USE ADATABASE

COPY TO BDATABASE FOR/WHILE &condition
```

determines the condition based on the FIELDS in the database ADATABASE. The following code determines the condition based on the last referenced field in CDATABASE:

```
SELE C
USE CDATABASE
SELE A
USE ADATABASE
COPY TO BDATABASE FOR C->&condition
```

This combination can provide for some useful conditional COPYs. Conditions can be precisely defined, and databases in several areas can be used.

COUNT	determines the number of records in the SELECTed database that match the condition.
DELETE	marks records to be DELETEd in the SELECTed database based on conditions in either the SELECTed or non-SELECTed database. The syntax for DELETEing records based on conditions set in non-SELECTED databases is similar to that used for the COPY command. The result can be some useful conditional deletions.
DISPLAY	sends user-defined information to the screen, one screenful at a time, based on user-defined conditions in the SELECTed or non-SELECTed database, or a combination of the two.
LABEL FORM	follows the syntax of DISPLAY
LIST	follows the syntax of DISPLAY
LOCATE	follows the syntax of DELETE
RECALL	follows the syntax of DELETE
REPLACE	follows the syntax of COPY
REPORT	follows the syntax of DISPLAY

APPEND and JOIN allow only the FOR qualifier but follow the syntax of COPY. All commands in this section can be further defined with the *NEXT n* qualifier.

II
Turnkey Systems with dBASE III

The time required to write a fully implemented turnkey system is often gauged in programmer-months; you can expect it to run to programmer-years. The reason is simple: you are writing a program that will do everything but turn the machine on and off.

Only rarely will a sole programmer undertake such a project. It involves creating multi-level error traps and text- and code-sensitive help screens. The program must be "forgiving" and, to some extent, even "intelligent." (Notice that I haven't even begun to talk about the code!)

Conversely, you shouldn't design and implement a turnkey system for one client, unless you will be paid incredibly well or are a martyr. Development time for the average turnkey system is 12 months. Getting all the bugs out will usually take another two years. By that time your customer(s) will be ready for an upgrade. You'll be ready for a padded cell.

A turnkey system is a program designed so completely that all the user does is activate the system. Every module has been planned to the smallest detail; accounting formulas, access menus, and databases have all been designed and implemented.

If you are hired to create a turnkey system for a client, prepare yourself for headaches, nausea, exhaustion, and incredible pressure. Because a turnkey system is an expensive purchase financially and psychologically, you will find that your client is more fastidious in choosing a system than in choosing a spouse.

This section deals with the theory of designing turnkey systems. If you have never before attempted such a system, use these rules as codes to live by:

JDI's Standard Rule of Programming # 12

Inertia controls programming. Once you start working on something, you can't stop. The project gets you out of bed in the morning and away from the dinner table in the evening. You may even find yourself writing notes in the tub. These things are true even after you finish the project.

JDI's Standard Rule of Programming # 13

When you are estimating how long a project will take, convert the estimated time period to the next larger unit and multiply by two. For example, if you think a project will take two weeks, give yourself four months:

2 weeks → 2 * 2 months

Months are the next higher time value. Convert weeks to months and multiply by two.

JDI's Standard Rule of Programming # 14

When you design a turnkey system, use Rule #13 and add 10. If you give yourself two months, the project will take 14 years:

2 months → (2 * 2) + 10 years

9
Hardware and Software Considerations

Inherent in the nomen *turnkey system* is the realization that you're not just responsible for writing a lot of code. You are also responsible for providing (or at least specifying) the computer hardware your programs will work with.

"Very good," you say. "The clients must use a PC, AT, or clone."

Wrong, I say. What size drives? Floppy or Hard disk? Do they need a streamer? A print spooler? A printer? A graphics printer or letter-quality? Or will a DMP suffice? How much memory? What type of memory? What kind of boards?

All of these are system considerations. If the system must have a printer, then the computer must either know that the printer is active or be ready to by-pass any error messages when they occur. The computer might also need to check RAM to make sure all memory is active and usable by the program, especially if the program creates its own RAMdisk or spooler. These things usually involve some non-dBASE III coding, so I merely mention that they must be considered; here, I discuss only those things that can be handled easily and don't require a book in themselves.

The CONFIG.SYS File

The CONFIG.SYS file plays a major role in any turnkey system (see Chapter 2). When you use the CONFIG.SYS file, you need to make sure that all system parameters and devices drivers are loaded. This is especially important if you plan to attach special equipment to the system.

For complete discussions on designing device drivers, read the IBM (or IBM-compatible) *Technical Reference*, and read thoroughly the *DOS Programmer's Reference.* Pay special attention to the sections about installing device drivers and the request header.

The AUTOEXEC.BAT File

After the computer has read the CONFIG.SYS file, DOS looks for AUTOEXEC.BAT files. This file initiates the work of the turnkey system's user interface. AUTOEXEC.BAT asks the user questions and passes the answers as parameters to lines further down. This program also checks system conditions and obtains date and time information from the system clock or the user.

The simplest turnkey system boots up automatically. The user simply places a disk in a drive and turns the computer on. The following example shows a simple AUTOEXEC.BAT file.

```
ECHO OFF
CHDIR\DBASE
PROMPT $P$G
BREAK ON
.
.
```

```
.     *************************************************************
.     *                                                           *
.     *                                                           *
.     *                                                           *
.     *                                                           *
.     *    PLEASE PLACE THE DBASE SYSTEM DISK IN DRIVE A          *
.     *                                                           *
.     *                                                           *
.     *                                                           *
.     *                                                           *
.     *************************************************************
.
.
PAUSE
DBASE master
```

The file name "master" identifies a master menu or program file that is executed as soon as dBASE III is loaded.

The AUTOEXEC.BAT file can perform a number of sophisticated functions before dBASE III is even loaded to the computer. You can test for the existence of certain files with code such as the following:

```
IF NOT EXIST *.dbf GOTO NODBF
 .
 .
 .
:NODBF
 . THE DATABASE FILES ARE MISSING.
 . PLEASE PLACE THE PROPER DISK IN DRIVE B:
PAUSE
IF NOT EXIST B:*.DBF GOTO NODBF
COPY B:*.DBF
```

This code also copies missing files to where they are needed. Note that the previous example uses a recursive command to ensure that the right disks are put in the drives.

The FOR command can be used with the IF command to guide the user with message files:

```
IF %1==JOSEPH GOTO JOSEPH
IF %1==DAN GOTO DAN
:JOSEPH
FOR %%A IN (M1.JDC,M2.JDC,M3.JDC,...) DO TYPE %%A
```

Although you have seen only a few examples, remember that BATch files have more applications in a turnkey system than those typical of the AUTOEXEC.BAT file.

Other BATch Files

Some programmers argue that BATch-file commands are a kind of programming language. Frankly, I don't care one way or the other. BATch files are useful tools that Microsoft designed for programmers, so let's spend some time studying them.

Turnkey systems are seldom left as they are; upgrades are inevitable. That fact and the fact of user's cyberphobia make a strong argument for the UPGRADE.BAT file. The majority of users will panic when an upgrade goes poorly and their $10,000 baby gets sick. The users will call you, usually at 2 a.m., to wail about the loss of their upgrade and the existing files. Usually, such a loss has not occurred; that is the user's fear, however.

The UPGRADE.BAT file should check whether the most recent update is on the disk. You can make the file perform such a check either by changing the name of the programs every time you upgrade the system or by performing an ERRORLEVEL check with a compiled subroutine. The subroutine might look for a flag in the program file. If the flag is not where it's supposed to be, then the upgrade is executed; if the flag is where it belongs, then nothing happens. Error code 0Eh is not used and can be set by a program if no update is necessary. A batch-file line that tests for that condition is

```
IF ERRORLEVEL 14 GOTO NOUPDATE
```

You can also pass parameters to the batch file by using the *%n* syntax. A check for valid disk drives would start with a message and then proceed as follows:

```
ECHO OFF
IF NOT TEST==%2TEST GOTO GOOD1
.
.        YOU DIDN'T TELL US WHICH DRIVE WE'RE WORKING WITH. TRY
.
.        AGAIN, AND SPECIFY DRIVE A:, B:, OR C: AS YOUR TARGET
```

```
GOTO END
:GOOD1
IF %1==%2 GOTO ONEISTWO
IF %1==A: GOTO GOOD2
IF %1==B: GOTO GOOD2
IF %1==C: GOTO GOOD2
  .
  .       YOU ONLY HAVE A:, B:, OR C: AVAILABLE
  .
GOTO END
:ONEISTWO
  .
  .       YOUR SOURCE DRIVE HAS TO BE DIFFERENT FROM YOUR TARGET DRIVE
  .
GOTO END
:GOOD2
COPY %1*.* %2
:END
```

Note: Not all versions of the BATch-file processor allow the use of the period in place of the REM command. Your listing will read more clearly if your version supports use of the period.

Notice that I test to see whether a drive has been selected (TEST==%1TEST) before I test the validity of the drive.

Another use of BATch files is to set up initial subdirectories for different users:

```
IF %1==2 GOTO TWO
IF %1==3 GOTO THREE
IF %1==4 GOTO FOUR
IF %1==5 GOTO FIVE
:TWO
FOR %%A IN (%2,%3) DO MD %%A
FOR %%A IN (%2,%3) DO COPY A:*.* \%%A
GOTO END
:THREE
FOR %%A IN (%2,%3,%4) DO MD %%A
FOR %%A IN (%2,%3,%4) DO COPY A:*.* \%%A
GOTO END
:FOUR
FOR %%A IN (%2,%3,%4,%5) DO MD %%A
FOR %%A IN (%2,%3,%4,%5) DO COPY A:*.* \%%A
GOTO END
```

```
:FIVE
FOR %%A IN (%2,%3,%4,%5,%6) DO MD %%A
FOR %%A IN (%2,%3,%4,%5,%6) DO COPY A:*.* \%%A
:END
```

You can start the preceding program from the DOS prompt by entering

```
SETUP 3 JOSEPH SUSAN JIM
```

The CONFIG.DB File and Turnkey Systems

The CONFIG.DB file is also important to a dBASE III turnkey system. dBASE III uses this file to set the operating parameters, many of which are the same as the SET ON/OFF commands. This file should be kept on the disk used to boot dBASE III.

Some important CONFIG.DB commands in the design of a turnkey system are ALTERNATE, COMMAND, DEBUG, DEFAULT, ESCAPE, F2 through F10, MAXMEM, MVARSIZ, PATH, and WP.

When the system is first set up, ALTERNATE should be both set and active. The initial setups always have some "bugs" that need to be fixed. With ALTERNATE active, all work done by the users will be captured. The de-bugging team will be able to recreate the errors that brought the system to a halt. You should keep the ALTERNATE file on a disk that can be sent back to the programming house if necessary. Once the turnkey system is running without problems, you can remove the command.

The COMMAND command provides a method of bypassing the AUTOEXEC.BAT command line *DBASE programname*. COMMAND gives you the option of placing the main program name in the CONFIG.DB file, and executing the program from there. If one main program performs all the jobs, this method works well. If, on the other hand, several sections reside on separate disks or in different directories, it is better to use the BATch-file method discussed earlier.

Another invaluable command is DEBUG. I suggest, however, that you slightly alter the command. It is more valuable if the CONFIG.SYS file sets up the system so that certain things ordinarily sent to the printer are instead sent to a disk file. DEBUG, used in this way, is very useful. The programmer can simply check the disk to find the problem, instead of looking through pages of print.

DEFAULT should be used only if database, index, format, and other files reside on a disk other than the one used to boot dBASE III. You should set ESCAPE to *off*, unless you want to let your clients quit the program in a way that you can't control. That is always a risky way to exit a program; it should be avoided. Valuable files might be damaged, and the integrity of data files is vital in any DBMS.

Later in this book, I describe how to program the function keys with dBASE III. You can also set these keys to initial values with the CONFIG.DB file. Then the function keys can be used to interrupt the programs, terminate execution, return to DOS, RUN programs external to dBASE III, or change modules.

MAXMEM tells dBASE III the amount of available memory within the computer. If there is enough memory space, dBASE III will set up larger files and buffers, place more data in memory, and write to disk less frequently. The good part of MAXMEM is that the command causes dBASE to run faster. The bad part is the more data you keep in memory, the more your data is susceptible to surges, spikes, and other power-supply problems. Another problem is that dBASE will use all the memory, so you will be unable to run a COM or EXE file external to dBASE.

MVARSIZ tells dBASE III how much room to allow for memory variables. This use of this command is entirely dependent on the application. If the application relies heavily on manipulation of memory variables and less on database work, allow a large share of memory for the variables. You can also store memory variables in an unused database area, eliminating the need for MEM files or memory variable allocations.

PATH is a useful command when necessary files are kept in subdirectories. Note that dBASE III searches the directory from which it was booted before searching any other. If dBASE finds the file name close to the original directory, the search stops there, even if the file isn't the correct one for the application.

Suppose, for example, that dBASE III resides in the subdirectory C:\dBases\d3, and that several auxiliary programs are in C:\dBases\d3\d3stuff. Your latest upgrade of TESTER.PRG is in the d3stuff subdirectory. An earlier unworking version is in subdirectory d3. Even though dBASE knows that a PATH exists to d3stuff, it will use the earlier version of TESTER.PRG when you DO TESTER.

If you plan to use memo fields often, WP is a useful command. In most applications, if you need to use word processing, you might be wiser simply to use

```
RUN wordprocessor
```

than to create MEMO fields.

The following CONFIG.DB file includes all of the commands I've explained. You can use these commands in any valid combination, such as

```
DEFAULT = C:
BELL = OFF
TALK = OFF
HEADINGS = OFF
SAFETY = OFF
DELIMITER = ON
DELIMITER = ><
CONFIRM = OFF
ALTERNATE = C:DEBUG
DEBUG = ON
EXACT = OFF
WP=STAR
MAXMEM=320
MVARSIZ=10
```

The CONFIG.DB file performs the following functions:

Command	*Function*
`DEFAULT = C:`	Set the default drive to C: (I normally work with an IBM PC/XT).
`BELL = OFF`	The BELL is extremely annoying, so shut it off. There are more civil methods to alert users of errors.
`TALK = OFF`	Don't bore or frighten the user by displaying everything dBASE does. Turn off that display with TALK.
`HEADINGS = OFF`	Turn off the HEADINGS and SAFETY so you can create your programs with headings and backup procedures.

SAFETY = OFF	See HEADINGS.
DELIMITER = ON DELIMITER = ><	DELIMITERS are a matter of personal choice, as previously mentioned.
CONFIRM = OFF	The programs handle most situations so you do not need to CONFIRM anything.
ALTERNATE = C:DEBUG DEBUG = ON	When customers call me with a problem, I ask them to send a copy of the DEBUG disk, so both DEBUG and ALTERNATE are listed.
EXACT = ON	I don't trust the user to remember exactly what was entered, so I instruct dBASE to find approximately, not EXACTLY, what the customer looked for.
WP=STAR	I use a modified version of WordStar.
MAXMEM=320	The system has 640k of RAM. I limit dBASE III to half that capacity with MAXMEM.
MVARSIZ=10	I use several active memory variables during the execution of my program. A MVARSIZ of 10k is should do the trick.

Now we've programmed for the computer and dBASE III. Despite the research that may be involved in these parts, they are the easiest parts of designing a turnkey system. After all, we can be fairly certain that the machine—which we either provide or specify—is not going to be changed or modified without our knowledge. Usually, Ashton-Tate is pretty good about letting the public know when they're going to monkey with dBASE. The next chapter introduces the tough parts.

10
Programming for Your Audience

This chapter returns to the psychology of the user. I base it not on studies, but on my 15 years' experience in performing variations on a theme.

Now that you have tools to assist you in your dBASE III programming, you should realize that the user doesn't care about the tools you use. Suppose you develop a slick system for accepting both numeric and alpha input from the user. This is all background programming to the user, who won't care a whit how you put the program together. You may have been hired for your background programming abilities, but they don't matter when the customer sits down to use your program.

When you are hired as a programmer, you need to spend time in the environment for which you are programming—especially if you are planning to attempt vertical-market software, which is dBASE III's strong point and every turnkey system's potential.

You may want to develop a menu screen like the one shown in figure 10.1. That's all well and good, as long as you keep in mind that the menu screen will only work in one office, and will work only because you know the owner of the business and because she has a sense of humor. The menu screen will not work in a vertical market application, even if the program works better than any other product on the market.

```
================================================================================
 ::                 M A I N   M E N U   P R O G R A M                        ::
--------------------------------------------------------------------------------
 ::                                                                          ::
 ::                                                                          ::
 ::                 0. EXIT TO DOS                                           ::
 ::                                                                          ::
 ::                 1. PERSONAL AUTO                                         ::
 ::                 2. COMMERCIAL AUTO                                       ::
 ::                 3. HOMEOWNMER                                            ::
 ::                 4. DISCREPANCY NOTICE                                    ::
 ::                 5. CONFIRMATION                                          ::
 ::                 6. MISCELLANEOUS                                         ::
 ::                 7. OPTION SEVEN NOT YET DEFINED                          ::
 ::                 8. OPTION EIGHT EQUALLY UNDEFINED                        ::
 ::                 9. SEE OPTION EIGHT                                      ::
 ::                                                                          ::
 ::                                                                          ::
 ::                                                                          ::
==========================SELECTION -> 0 ========================================
->
```

Fig. 10.1. A menu screen.

The next consideration is that you may enjoy being the hired gun, "The Pro from Dover." Hired guns are impressive, but only when others have already been working for some time at the problem the "gun" is hired to kill. They've done most of the work. You can be effective in this capacity because of your distance from the problem and because of your wider experience.

Yes, it's nice to be a pro. Say hello to JDI's Standard Programming Rule #22:

If you design a program for one group, you're paid once. If you design a program for an environment, you are paid over and over again.

I first hinted at this fact when I suggested that you program in modules and tasks in order to build a library. Once you've built the library, the magic is easy. The real magic, however, comes from linking the library modules so they can be used in several similar environments, also called *vertical markets*.

I have found that the only way to know a market is to spend time in it. A good start is to spend some time interviewing clients and staff. The main menu shown earlier works well in one particular office, but the same menu would not necessarily work in all similar offices.

You need to determine how much work you can transport from one environment to the next. Ponds are all small bodies of water, but they contain different organisms depending on where they are in the world. The insurance industry is an example: Some things are unique to east-coast agencies, and are not used anywhere else in the country.

Your immediate audience is the client who pays your bill, so pay primary attention to his or her needs. Also remember that your fee will not keep you in kippers very long and that you will have to eat next month, too. Can this environment's work be carried elsewhere?

Now you have determined your audience and have started to code. Most clients are very particular about the way the program works. They will tell you how they want the information to appear on-screen and in print, how they want to access data, who can manipulate data, and so on. Pay careful attention to their wishes and make them a priority. Unless you've spent time in their environment, your clients know the industry better than you do. And after all, they are paying your salary, so they know better than you do even when they don't.

Before You Begin

I consider a file-check subroutine mandatory, in a turnkey system. Other programmers, however, often overlook this step. I like to know that I have all the pieces before I put a puzzle together. Nobody wants to get half done with a puzzle and suddenly find part of a tree or, even worse, part of a face missing. This same rule applies to dBASE III. The same is true for having all necessary files available when the program begins.

Why would I need to make sure all the files are available? Because once upon a time, two people in two separate locations decided to learn DOS by ERASEing some necessary files.

My file-checking routine uses its own database, FILECHEK, with the following structure:

```
Structure for database  : C:FILECHEK.DBF
Number of data records  :       28
Date of last update     : 11/30/84
Field  Field name  Type        Width    Dec
1  FILENAME    Character     12
** Total **                        13
```

The routine itself is short and direct:

```
USE FILECHEK
? "Missing files"
DO WHILE .NOT. EOF()
**
     IF .NOT. FILE('&FILENAME')
          ? FILENAME
     ENDIF
**
     SKIP
ENDDO
```

Improvements to this routine might include the ability to check other directories and disks. The completed version might be as follows:

```
USE FILECHEK
FINDFILE=FILENAME
DO WHILE .NOT. EOF()
     IF FILE('&FINDFILE')
          SKIP
          FINDFILE=FILENAME
          LOOP
     ELSE
          CLEAR
          ? FINDFILE+' NOT FOUND.'
          ? 'NEW PATH [DN:\DIRECTORY\(DIRECTORY\...)]'
          ? 'NEW DISK [PLEASE TYPE THE DISK DRIVE (A:, B:, C:,...)]'
          ? 'SKIP TO NEXT FILE [S]'
          ACCE 'YOUR CHOICE -> 'TO CHOICE
          IF UPPER(CHOICE)='S'
               SKIP
               FINDFILE=FILENAME
               LOOP
          ENDIF
```

```
            FINDFILE=CHOICE+FINDFILE
            IF .NOT. FILE('&FINDFILE')
                 LOOP
            ELSE
                 RUN COPY &FINDFILE
                 SKIP
                 FINDFILE=FILENAME
            ENDIF
       ENDIF
ENDDO
```

This routine places on the user's shoulders some of the burden of specifying search paths. The entire subroutine could be coded in BASIC. In BASIC, however, the data file would be a straight ASCII file, FILENAME.TXT:

```
DB3-01.BAK
MYNAME.JOE
HERNAME.SLK
WHATELSE.IS
THERE
DB3-01.DB3
DB3-01.2
```

The BASIC program is equally simple:

```
5 REM FILECHEK.BAS
10 OPEN "FILENAME.TXT" FOR INPUT AS 1
20 ON ERROR GOTO 100
30 WHILE NOT EOF(1)
40      INPUT#1,FILE$
50      OPEN FILE$ FOR INPUT AS 2
60      CLOSE#2
70      REM
80 WEND
90 SYSTEM
100 IF ERL=50 THEN PRINT FILE$;" MISSING"
110 RESUME 70
```

Both the dBASE III and BASIC routines are elegantly simplistic. Just remember to customize.

Setting the Function Keys to Rule the World

Another helpful routine redefines the function keys. F1 is permanently set to call up the dBASE III HELP screens. F2 through F10 are ours to use, however, and with a little ingenuity we can even claim F1 for our own use.

F2 through F10 can be redefined to send arbitrary character strings, which is an excellent quality when you are working for someone else. Remember that the users would rather use the function keys than the keyboard.

For example, you can redefine the function keys to send the simple character strings

E for EDIT
N for SKIP (as in NEXT RECORD)
B for SKIP -1 (as in BACK 1 RECORD)
D for DELETE

Because dBASE has etched F1 in stone, we place our redefinitions on the bottom keys:

F7 → B F8 → N
F9 → E F10 → D

A preliminary sketch of the code for the screen would appear as follows:

```
                                           +============================+
SET COLOR TO 5+                            |+==========================+|
@ 10,Ø SAY 'F1 -> HELP  F2 ->        ' ||                          ||
@ 11,Ø SAY 'F3 ->       F4 ->        ' ||         M E N U          ||
@ 12,Ø SAY 'F5 ->       F6 ->        ' ||                          ||
@ 13,Ø SAY 'F7 -> BACK  F8 -> NEXT'    ||        B L O C K         ||
@ 14,Ø SAY 'F9 -> EDIT  F1Ø ->DELE'    ||                          ||
                                           |+==========================+|
                                           +============================+
```

Note: The MENU BLOCK is not a part of the code above. The block is simply a symbol that more code will eventually fill that space.

This method requires writing much more code than you need just to get the job done, but this is the other side of the balance mentioned earlier. In this case, the other side of the balance is ease of use for the customer, which must be a priority. What exactly is the balance? You've no doubt noticed that I stress keeping code as compact as possible and only coding what is necessary to get a job done. Here I say to go to any length imaginable to code for the customer, which means to write lots of code that might never be used if the customer never creates an error condition.

With a little premeditation the following program, MENUCALL.PRG, can be adapted to a variety of environments. It creates a colorful function-key default box.

```
***MENUCALL.PRG
***BY JOSEPH-DAVID CARRABIS, JDI, INC., HANOVER, NH 03755
**
PUBLIC KEYWORD2, KEYWORD3, KEYWORD4, KEYWORD5
PUBLIC KEYWORD6, KEYWORD7, KEYWORD8, KEYWORD9
PUBLIC RECNUM, MENUNAME
SET PROCEDURE TO FKEYFILE
**
MENUNAME="TEST"
DO ASSGNKEY
**
DO WHILE .T.
DO MENUSHEL
DO MENUFILL WITH RECNUM
DO FCNKEY WITH RECNUM
WAIT
ENDDO
```

Because I have mentioned procedure files so often, I felt obligated to use them here. All the DO's in MENUCALL.PRG are found in the procedure file FKEYFILE.PRG.

```
***FKEYFILE.PRG PROCEDURE FILE FOR FUNCTION KEY BASED MENU GENERATORS
***BY JOSEPH-DAVID CARRABIS, JDI, INC. HANOVER, NH 03755
**
PROCEDURE ASSGNKEY
SELECT 10
USE KEYVALUE
LOCATE FOR KEYFIELD="&MENUNAME"
SKIP
STORE RECNO() TO HERE, RECNUM
THERE=HERE+8
N=2
```

```
DO WHILE HERE<THERE
   GOTO HERE
   KEYFUNC='KEYWORD'+STR(N,1,Ø)
   STORE KEYDESCRP TO &KEYFUNC
   SET FUNCTION N TO TRIM(KEYFIELD)
   N=N+1
   HERE=HERE+1
ENDDO
SET FUNCTION 1Ø TO "EXIT;"
RETURN
**
PROCEDURE MENUSHEL
CLEAR
TEXT
======================================================================
||                      M E N U   S Y S T E M                       ||
======================================================================
||                                                                  ||
|| F1-> HELP F2->       |F1=> ACTIVATE THE DBASE III HELP MENU SYSTEM ||
||                      |F2=>                                       ||
|| F3->      F4->       |F3=>                                       ||
||                      |F4=>                                       ||
|| F5->      F6->       |F5=>                                       ||
||                      |F6=>                                       ||
|| F7->      F8->       |F7=>                                       ||
||                      |F8=>                                       ||
|| F9->      FØ-> EXIT  |F9=>                                       ||
||                      |FØ=> EXIT TO DBASE III                     ||
======================================================================
ENDTEXT
RETURN
**
PROCEDURE MENUFILL
PARAMETER HERE
SET COLOR TO 2+
@  5,17 SAY KEYWORD2
@  7, 7 SAY KEYWORD3
@  7,17 SAY KEYWORD4
@  9, 7 SAY KEYWORD5
@  9,17 SAY KEYWORD6
@ 11, 7 SAY KEYWORD7
@ 11,17 SAY KEYWORD8
@ 13, 7 SAY KEYWORD9
```

```
SET COLOR TO W, ,
N=6
THISHERE=HERE
THERE=HERE+8
SELECT 10
DO WHILE THISHERE<THERE
   GOTO THISHERE
   @ N,27 SAY WHATITDOES
   THISHERE=THISHERE+1
   N=N+1
ENDDO
RETURN
**
PROCEDURE FCNKEY
PARAMETER HERE
SELECT 10
@ 22,0
WAIT "YOUR CHOICE -> " TO KEYIN
KEYIN=ASC(KEYIN)
   DO CASE
      CASE KEYIN=254
         GOTO HERE+1
         DOIT=COMMAND
         &DOIT
      CASE KEYIN=253
         GOTO HERE+2
         DOIT=COMMAND
         &DOIT
      CASE KEYIN=252
         GOTO HERE+3
         DOIT=COMMAND
         &DOIT
      CASE KEYIN=251
         GOTO HERE+4
         DOIT=COMMAND
         &DOIT
      CASE KEYIN=250
         GOTO HERE+5
         DOIT=COMMAND
         &DOIT
```

```
      CASE KEYIN=249
         GOTO HERE+6
         DOIT=COMMAND
         &DOIT
      CASE KEYIN=248
         GOTO HERE+7
         DOIT=COMMAND
         &DOIT
      CASE KEYIN=247
         GOTO HERE+8
         DOIT=COMMAND
         &DOIT
      CASE KEYIN=246
         CANCEL
   ENDCASE
RETURN
**
***END OF FKEYFILE.PRG PROCEDURE FILE
```

The joy of using MENUCALL.PRG and FKEYFILE.PRG is that they make it easy to alter function keys. The database file, KEYVALUE, has the following structure:

```
Structure for database : C:KEYVALUE.dbf
Number of data records :       11
Date of last update    : 01/01/80
Field  Field name  Type        Width    Dec
1  KEYFIELD    Character    100
2  KEYDESCRP   Character      4
3  WHATITDOES  Character     40
4  COMMAND     Character     20
** Total **                     165
```

Note: In these routines I did not redefine the dBASE III HELP key assignment (F1), and I included an EXIT key assignment at F10.

How does the whole shebang work? Let's start with the database file. KEYFIELD stores a command line that is assigned to a key. For example, F2 can be redefined to

```
DISP STRUC; WAIT; DISP MEMO; WAIT; DISP STAT; WAIT; DISP ALL;
```

The semicolons represent carriage returns in the command line. You may think it is unnecessary to display all those things. I agree. I have, however, found a need to assign such things as

```
SELECT 2; FIND &VAR; DO [FORMAT FILE]; DO [GETTER FILE]; READ;
```

Now that is a worthy command line! It demonstrates some of the flexibility of the function keys. The FORMAT and GETTER files mentioned in the example are merely files that paint the screen (FORMAT) and then retrieve information for the memory or the database (GETTER).

KEYDESCRP holds the four-letter mnemonic that I use to fill in the menu next to each function-key assignment. WHATITDOES becomes the actual MENU line that describes each key's function.

Now I'll show you some devious programming.

Notice that I include the database field COMMAND. I include COMMAND as a database field because I can assign a short, one-line command to that field. That executable command is then read to a variable:

```
DOIT=COMMAND
```

Then I execute the command with

```
&DOIT
```

in PROCEDURE FCNKEY.

Essentially, I have given the function keys two sets of definitions. I place one set of definitions with the command line

```
SET FUNCTION N TO TRIM(KEYFIELD)
```

The line can be as long as memory allows because of the use of the semicolon, which works as a carriage return in the command line. Those function-key definitions remain until the keys are reassigned.

The other set of definitions, which is taken from the COMMAND field, can be used immediately. These definitions are shorter than the KEYFIELD definitions because you cannot insert RETURNs in a macro statement with the semicolon, CHR(13), or CHR(13)+CHR(10).

The PROCEDURE FCNKEY subroutine uses an interesting feature. You can use the line

```
WAIT TO variablename
```

to place the function-key assignments in variables without executing them. The ASC( ) values of the keys are listed in Appendix J.

I have one more routine that I have not included in the FKEYFILE PROCEDURE file. I place the routine at various points in my programs, wherever I need it. Because of the way I use the routine, I can't guarantee that the proper procedure file is open at the time the routine is called. This routine simply changes the function key values on the fly.

```
***CHNGEKEY.PRG
***
ANOTHER=.T.
DO WHILE ANOTHER
CLEAR
NEWDEF=SPACE(80)
INPU "Which key do you want to change (2,3,...10)? -> " TO NEWKEY
     ? "Enter the new key definition below"
@ 5,0 GET NEWDEF
@ 20,0 SAY "Do another (Y/N)? -> " GET ANOTHER
READ
SET FUNCTION NEWKEY TO TRIM("&NEWDEF")
ENDDO
```

I know what you're thinking: "This is all well and good, but what does it really do, JD?" You can use these routines to design turnkey systems that, with the exception of data entry and manipulation, are controlled completely from the function keys. Impressive and nice.

Displaying Help Screens

Recognize that users are not as sophisticated as you'd like them to be. Your clients will freeze at the keyboard for no apparent reason, and if help is not available at the keyboard, they will call you for help.

Fortunately, dBASE III makes it possible to help the user without clouding the program with unnecessary code. The method is to create a database of MEMO fields, each record containing help screens for different parts of the program. As each module is accessed, it positions a pointer to the corresponding help-screen database. Now the program can set one of the function keys to the string

```
SELE J;GOTO recordnumber of help screens;DISP help screen fields;
```

so that the user has easy access to the help screens at all times.

Note: Make sure the memo fields are no more than 22 lines long. This prevents the help message from rolling off the screen.

An alternative method is to set one of the keys to

```
CLEAR; DO HELPER WITH PROGNUM;
```

The HELPER module is a subroutine with a PARAMETER command that passes PROGNUM, the calling program's number. PROGNUM is a variable which changes according to which module is in USE. The database is similar to the one described in the preceding paragraph, except that a numeric field is used for INDEXing purposes, and that one record contains all the help screens for a particular section. The HELPER program becomes

```
PARAMETER CALLER
SELE J
USE HELPSCRN INDEX CALLER
FIND &CALLER
SELE I
USE HSSTRUC                ** A STRUC file corresponding to the
**                            help screen database file
DO WHILE .NOT. EOF()
     FIELD=FIELD_NAME
     SELE J
     DISP &FIELD
     WAIT "(C)ontinue, any other key to exit" TO MORE
     IF UPPER(MORE) <> "C"
          RETURN
     ENDIF
     SELE I
     SKIP
ENDDO
**
RETURN
```

The structure file serves as a counter of the help screens in the example. When the last help screen has been DISPLAYed, HELPER RETURNs to the calling program. After reading the information, the user can RETURN by pressing any key except C. A possible improvement is to use the REPORT command to add the ability to print the help screens.

Note: When MEMO fields are passed through the REPORT command, the listings are fifty characters wide.

In the last section, we discussed coding for both the computer and dBASE III. This section involved coding for the user. The sheer length of the section and number of topics discussed should indicate which of the two jobs is harder.

A closing monologue about coding for your audience: Users aren't as sophisticated as you are. If they were, they would write their own code or at least help you when you code. Because they aren't as sophisticated, be careful and gentle. Remember the prof who used to fill a board with equations and say, "It's intuitively obvious to the casual observer . . ."? Don't do that to your clients. The easier the system is to use, the more likely you'll be able to sell it elsewhere. And—let's face it—aesthetics won't pay your rent.

11
dBASE III in the Office Environment

When a program is written for a working office, unique problems arise. They usually have little to do with the programmatic aspect of dBASE III; they deal more with dBASE III's integration into the office and with the work habits of the office staff. You must acknowledge that people make mistakes (and usually during data entry), realize that dBASE III is not the only program on the disk, and recognize that more than one person may want to use the computer at the same time.

Creating Error Traps and Loops

dBASE III's TYPE( ) function tells us the variable type and the validity of a CONDITION with regard to the database in USE and the referenced variable. This ability to determine the validity of a user-defined condition provides an error-checking method that is applicable in many turnkey systems. Unfortunately, the TYPE( ) command is poorly documented, as was TYPE( )'s dBASE II predecessor, TEST( ).

You can use TYPE( ) to determine whether the type of a memory variable is CHARACTER, LOGICAL, NUMERIC, or DATE. Remember that you cannot use MEMO variables because TYPE( ) works with memory variables, not field types.

Before you design an error trap using TYPE( ), you need to sit down at the computer and study the properties of the command. Start by designing a database as follows:

```
Structure for database  : C:CUSTOMERS.dbf
Number of data records  :       5
Date of last update     : 07/31/85
Field  Field name  Type        Width    Dec
1  FIRSTNAME   Character     30
2  LASTNAME    Character     30
3  ADDRESS     Character     30
4  CITY        Character     30
5  STATE       Character      2
6  ZIPCODE     Character     10
7  PHONE       Numeric       10
** Total **                     143
```

If you enter the line

```
? TYPE('FIRSTNAME')
```

you get *C* as a result because FIRSTNAME is declared in memory as a CHARACTER variable. For this example, you would use

```
? TYPE('FIRSTNAME="Joseph-David"')
```

and get *L* because that is a logical use of the variable type. If you enter

```
? TYPE('FIRSTNAME=29.33')
```

you receive a *U* because that is an illogical (or Unknown) use of the variable type.

In a program, this error check becomes

```
ACCE "Locate condition -> " TO condition
IF TYPE('&condition')="U"
     ? "That is an invalid condition."
     WAIT
     LOOP
ENDIF
```

The same error loop with a CASE command would appear as

```
ACCE "Locate condition -> " TO condition
**
DO CASE
   CASE TYPE('&condition)="U"
      ? "That is an invalid condition."
      WAIT
      EXIT
```

As a programmer, you must make sure the user can escape if a condition cannot be met. You need to offer the user the option of looping to the error check a number of times or exiting without harming other files.

The option of looping to an error check a number of times can best be handled by including a counter with the error message. After a number of unsuccessful attempts, the program might pull up a text-sensitive help screen, written either as a TEXT . . .ENDTEXT environment or as a specific MEMO field in a database of error messages. If an input error indicates denied access, you want to drop the user back to DOS without harming files. Simply QUITting dBASE should be enough to preserve database integrity. You may wish to use a CLOSE DATABASE command, just to be sure. For examples of the TYPE( ) command as an error check, see Appendixes D through H.

Making a Multiuser Environment with dBASE III

This section deals with pure theory and opens with a warning:

> At the time of the writing of this book, Ashton-Tate does not support a multiuser dBASE III system. Members of Ashton-Tate's technical support staff have said that a multiuser dBASE III is under development. This chapter deals purely with creating a kludge that works. In the best interest of your application, you might be wise to wait for the real product rather than attempt in practice what is discussed here in theory.

I do not recommend the following techniques for programmers with the least hesitancy or insecurity about their work. (That is a fairly good description of myself.) I learned the following techniques by sitting down with my own system for a month and experimenting. If the need arises, I suggest you do the same. Also note that this method has been used only on hard disk systems with at least twenty megabytes of disk space.

A multiuser system is a system that more than one individual can use at one time. Ideally, a multiuser system also supports multitasking, the ability to do more than one program at the same time. In any case, DOS provides a starting point for the former.

Let's consider a situation in which a number of users need to have access to a system, and their work needs to be kept separate. Don't worry about what the users are accessing; concern yourself only with the fact that each user's files have to be kept separate from other users' files at least part of the time. There are two ways to keep them separate.

One method is to use temporary files, perhaps numbered after each user's station. For example, consider the following code segment.

```
CLEAR
ACCE "What station is this (1,2,3,4 or 5)?  " TO STATION
CLIENTFL="CLTEMP"+STATION
PLCYFILE="PLCYTMP"+STATION
USE &CLIENTFL
SELE B
USE &PLCYFILE
ZAP
APPE BLAN
DO CLFRAME
```

Here, dBASE III creates temporary files as needed.

Another method of naming temporary files would be to use a truncation of the masterbase name concatenated to the user's station number.

In either case, this method is fine, provided you remember to delete all temporary files at the end of a work session and never to have more than 512 files in a directory. DOS will not handle more than 512 files in a directory.

The other method works by creating subdirectories for each worker. The system needs to be set up with DOS subdirectories, one corresponding to the individuals whose access must be kept separate. This can be easily achieved with a BATch file such as that shown in the section on BATch files (see Chapter 10).

Next, recognize that in order for you to create a multiuser system with a minimum of sweat, your clients must have purchased a commercial network software package. Which package your customers purchase is not relevant, but I suggest that they purchase elsewhere unless your house is in the business of writing and designing system software.

A list of interrupts for the networking software can be found in the software documentation or obtained from the company's support people. This list is made available to developers for their own use. The rest of this discussion relies heavily on the use of the network's system interrupt set.

The dBASE III files needed to get dBASE up and running (EXE, OVL) can be loaded in the subdirectories. Make sure you have enough disk space for all users. The dBASE system disk can be kept in the floppy drive or, if you have one of the new releases of dBASE III, tucked away for safe keeping.

The database, index, and memofield (DBT) files should be loaded into the main directory, from which all the other directories are accessed. The networking software may have sophisticated enough PATHing facilities for dBASE III's PATH= and SET PATH TO commands to find the necessary files no matter where they are. If not, you can get other commercially available utility programs that set search paths over DOS. Examples are dPATH, DOSPATH, and IBM File Facility. You must make sure that the necessary files are accessible to dBASE III.

Set up each subdirectory with database templates that correspond to all the database-indexfile combinations in the main directory.

In a compilable language (preferably an assembler), write a program that checks the interrupts. When any database is in use, return a nonzero value from the interrupt. Return a zero (0) when no databases are in use. Write the program so that it holds itself (and hence dBASE III) in a loop until the databases are freed for the next user.

After the databases are freed for use, copy the necessary information from the main directory databases to the templates in the subdirectory. This simple method can be used to prevent collisions when accessing databases and can be invoked with the dBASE III RUN command.

An important restriction is that information be pulled from the main directory databases into the subdirectory templates. This practice keeps main database access to a minimum and frees the databases for other users. Updating the main directory databases should be an end-of-day function because this work may tie up the main directory databases for a long time. If this time is unsatisfactory, have the main databases updated after each modification of the data in the templates. That leads us to the next warning:

> The essential goal in using a multiuser dBASE III system is to prevent record collisions. A collision occurs only if two or more users try to write to the same record at the same time; hence the suggestion that you hold information in separate subdirectory databases and write back to the main database at the end of the day. Problems with two or more users writing over each other's data are still possible. Unless separate subdirectory databases are maintained, the best way around that problem is to bully the office staff.

Running Other Programs under dBASE III

You don't always need to develop an entire system application with dBASE III because there are many software packages available. The packages may perform 90 percent of the functions your customers need, and you can add the other 10 percent by making slight modifications to the program.

One way to get the other 10 percent is to open the package. This method is usually unsatisfactory for several reasons:

1. At best, you can only decompile the package. If you're not comfortable with assemblers and reverse compilers, decompilation can be painfully intimidating.
2. You are forced to follow someone else's logic, which is virtually impossible. Nobody else thinks the way you do, and you don't think the way anyone else does.
3. You will make the warranties invalid. The warranties may or may not be enforceable, but the manufacturer can refuse you assistance unless you're a value-added dealer.
4. When you are finished, no one else can modify the program without going through the same headaches you went through.
5. The bugs in your work will show up at the *worst possible time.*

The other method, which negates all the objections listed (and most others I've encountered), is to program the desired functions using dBASE III. Usually, when another package is the primary use package, the only other necessary function is to massage the data in whatever ways the primary package is unable to do. Just remember that dBASE III can read files in many more formats than the usual SDF. Provided you know the file structure, and the data is ASCII text, you can program the primary program's file delimiters into a dBASE III search routine. Such a routine would first scan for a delimiter, then check the ASCII value of the next character. If the next character is text, take it and place it into some other database file, then continue to the next delimiter. If not, check for the next delimiter.

The question arises of how you determine another program's datafile structure. If the primary-use package is capable of writing and reading ASCII text files, you don't have to perform this step. Both the primary-use package and dBASE III can work with ASCII files, with dBASE III accessing them as SDF files. But what if the primary-use package can't read and write ASCII text files?

The answer is to use the DOS DEBUG program to determine the datafile's structure. Once that is done you can write a dBASE III program to read the other program's data, as mentioned above, and reverse the process slightly to write data back to a usable file.

Another question arises: how do you make the primary-use package comfortable with dBASE III? Fortunately, dBASE III allows you to RUN other programs, provided you have more than 256K of memory. This fact is a strong argument for having more than the minimum memory; it also provides an easier access to external programs (and the primary-use package) for your client.

Using dBASE III as an Umbrella

What does an umbrella have to do with dBASE III? The term *umbrella* refers to the capability of dBASE III to act as an integrator for a series of software packages.

For example, let's say you have a customer with several different packages on disk. dBASE, however, is the turnkey system and the backbone of the entire application. The users know the call names for the individual packages and are aware that arguments must be passed to the packages. Hence you only need to code a menu selection, such as

```
9 -> RUN ANOTHER PROGRAM
```

with follow-up code such as

```
CASE response=9
     CLEAR
     ACCE "What program do you wish to run? " TO program
     arguments=SPACE(50)
     ACCE "With? " TO arguments
     RUN &program &arguments
```

Most errors that cause the other program to trash will only leave the user inside dBASE.

A better example of dBASE III as umbrella entails assigning different programs to each of the function keys, as in figure 11.1. You can use this method to pass SDF files back and forth between programs. If you are extremely industrious, you can take the time to find out how various programs set up their work files. Don't bother. Most programs can write their working files as ASCII text files. If you use that capability, you can guarantee minimum work for yourself and maximum flexibility in system design.

Running a Word Processor under dBASE III

Most word processors work according to set rules. One rule is that you can use the DOS TYPE command to display a word-processing document on the monitor. The document may contain some garbage characters, as a WordStar document does, or it may be pure ASCII text.

In either case, you need to create a two-way street in order to RUN a word processor under dBASE III. You need to get information from dBASE to the word processor for merging (see Appendix F), and you need to move information from the word processor back to dBASE III.

At some point, your customers may wish to pull information from a document to a database. This transfer of information is not difficult if

1. The database has already been designed, and you can instruct the users in its basic structure.

```
================================================================================
-!!                    DBASE III UMBRELLA PROCESSOR                          !!
--------------------------------------------------------------------------------
!!                                                                           !!
!!         F1   ->   WORD PROCESSOR 1  (WORDSTAR)                            !!
!!         F2   ->   WORD PROCESSOR 2  (SAMNA)                               !!
!!         F3   ->   ACCOUNTING        (REAL WORLD)                          !!
!!         F4   ->   SPREADSHEET       (LOTUS 1-2-3)                         !!
!!         F5   ->   CALL BOSTON       (MITE TO HOME OFFICE)                 !!
!!         F6   ->   CALL NEW YORK     (MITE TO REGIONAL OFFICE)             !!
!!                                                                           !!
!!                                                                           !!
!!         F9   ->   DATABASE WORK     (DBASE III)                           !!
!!         F0   ->   QUIT                                                    !!
!!                                                                           !!
!!                                                                           !!
================================================================================
```

Fig. 11.1. Menu screen for an umbrella system.

2. You and the users agree ahead of time on a datafield DELIMITER.

3. You agree on a "flag" string. The flag string is any group of characters that you use to tell dBASE III that the following lines are not text, but data to be included in the database file.

When the three conditions are met, you are ready to write the program. Assume that you have created a document entitled 10JUN85.LTR and a database called JUN10VAL. The users know that the flag is a string of three asterisks (***) and the DELIMITER is a comma (,). The result is shown in figure 11.2.

```
To: The Word Processing Division
From: The dBASE III Division
Re: The information you requested

This letter will demonstrate the dBASE III program used to
strip text from a letter or other document and get it into the
required format for inclusion in a dBASE III database file. The
thing to note is that a "flag" is used. The requested data comes
before and after. The flag is "***".
***
Joseph   Carrabis  Hanover    NH
Jack     Jickjock  ManchesterNH
Someone  Else      Another    ST
Someone  In        PEI        CN
Ablast   from the  Past       2
Joseph   Carrabis  Hanover    NH
Jack     Jickjock  ManchesterNH
Someone  Else      Another    ST
Someone  In        PEI        CN
Ablast   from the  Past       2
***

->
->
->
```

Fig. 11.2. Delimiters marking data for extraction from a text file.

```
USE JUN10VAL
APPEND FROM 10JUN85.LTR SDF DELIM WITH ,
GOTO TOP
DO WHILE .NOT.EOF()
     IF FIELD1<>"***"
          DELE
          SKIP
          LOOP
```

```
    ELSE
        DELE
        SKIP
        DO WHILE .NOT. EOF()
            IF FIELD1<>"***"
                SKIP
                LOOP
            ELSE
                RECNUM=RECNO()
                EXIT
        ENDDO
        DELE
        GOTO RECNUM+1
    ENDIF
ENDDO
PACK
```

With this routine, you can move information from a file to a database file, even if the word processor does not use pure ASCII. The result of running the preceding program is shown in figure 11.3. If you analyze the code, you can see that the entire document is copied to the database. The flags indicate the beginning and the end of data for the database. Only the records between the flags are kept. All other records are DELETEd and PACKed when the code is completed.

1	Joseph	Carrabis	Hanover	NH
2	Jack	Jickjock	Manchester	NH
3	Someone	Else	Another	ST
4	Someone	In	PEI	CN
5	Ablast	from the	Past	2
6	Joseph	Carrabis	Hanover	NH
7	Jack	Jickjock	Manchester	NH
8	Someone	Else	Another	ST
9	Someone	In	PEI	CN
10	Ablast	from the	Past	2

Fig. 11.3. Data extracted from a text file.

Running A Spreadsheet Under dBASE III

Most spreadsheet programs can use files other than their standard work files. dBASE III uses this feature with the SDF file format. Many spreadsheets are on the market for the user and the system designer. In this discussion, I deal with Lotus 1-2-3, which seems to be the favorite of the industry.

Two problems are addressed here: getting information *to* and *from* 1-2-3, using dBASE III. 1-2-3 (and every other spreadsheet I've seen) can read standard ASCII files if delimiters are given. 1-2-3 needs to know if the incoming files are text or numeric input.

Next, we need to determine the client's needs. If the client needs to import an entire file to a starting cell on the spreadsheet, the command

```
COPY TO TOLOTUS.PRN SDF
```

will do the job. (You need to add the PRN extension so that 1-2-3 can import and export the files.)

If the database has several different fields, each record is written on a single line. 1-2-3 interprets the line as text. For example, a 500-record database with twenty fields per record becomes a 500-line, one-cell spreadsheet. The cell will be many characters long, but only one cell wide. This method of importing data to a spreadsheet is usually unsatisfactory.

An easier way to import files is to create separate PRN files on each field in the database and then to import them separately. The following program can generate importable files:

```
***LOTUSER.PRG -> dBASE III TO LOTUS 1-2-3 CONVERTER
PARAM database
**
USE &database
COPY STRUC EXTE TO STRCFILE
SELE J
USE STRCFILE
GOTO TOP
**
```

```
DO WHILE .NOT. EOF()
   fieldname=FIELD_NAME
   file=TRIM(SUBSTR(fieldname,1,6))+".PRN"
   SELE A
   COPY TO &file FIELDS &fieldname SDF
   SELE J
   SKIP
ENDDO
ERASE STRCFILE.DBF
RUN COPY *.PRN \LOTUS
RETURN
```

You invoke the program with the command line

```
DO LOTUSER WITH "databasefile"
```

where "databasefile" is the name of the database to be converted into a Lotus file. LOTUSER gets the name of the database to translate as a passed PARAMETER when first called.

The program then COPYs the EXTENDED STRUCTURE of the database to a temporary file called STRCFILE. After SELECTing STRCFILE and positioning itself, LOTUSER creates files to import to 1-2-3 from the FIELDNAMEs of STRCFILE. Each PRN file is named for the corresponding dBASE III database FIELDNAME, and the values of that field are COPYed to it. The program is repeated until STRCFILE has no more FIELDNAMEs to process.

From within 1-2-3, all you have to do is set up some autoloading macros. These macros depend to a great extent on the sophistication of your client. If you can trust your client to place the cursor where the data needs to go on the spreadsheet, you simply need to autoload the macro

```
/FIT
```

This is not a difficult procedure. Assume that you plan to label the MACRO "I" for "import," and you want to place the MACRO at a remote cell of the spreadsheet.

```
/RNC\I
AA100
[F5] AA100       ** Press the F5 (GOTO) key, then type
'AA100'
'/FI'
```

Now the user need only supply an argument—T(ext) or N(umbers)—and the name of the file to be imported, which will appear at the top of the spreadsheet.

But what about the unsophisticated user? First, assume that you are going to use the same type of database to create importable files for 1-2-3. The LOTUSER program can still do the job, but you need to add a more sophisticated macro to the 1-2-3 spreadsheet. This macro would be more complicated:

```
/FITprnfile1~{RIGHT}/FITprnfile2~{RIGHT}/FITprnfile3~{RIGHT}...
```

Ns are used in place of *Ts* if the PRN file is NUMERIC and not TEXT data.

This macro "assumes" that the client can move the cursor to the first data entry cell but this is not always the case. The last part of this macro string might be

```
{GOTO} starting address
```

if the starting point cell for data entry is always the same.

As a last example, let's consider variations that make dBASE III generate an importable file from any dBASE databases. The LOTUSER program can handle that job with only a few modifications. After the program exits the DO WHILE . . . ENDDO loop, change the program code to the following:

```
GOTO TOP
REPLACE ALL FIELD_NAME WITH TRIM(SUBSTR(FIELD_NAME,1,6))+".PRN"
REPLACE ALL FIELD_TYPE WITH "T" FOR FIELD_TYPE="C"
COPY TO FIELDS.PRN FIELDS FIELD_NAME SDF
COPY TO TYPES.PRN FIELDS FIELD_TYPE SDF
RUN COPY *.PRN \LOTUS
RETURN
```

With these modifications, you can import files that provide variables for 1-2-3's macro programming facilities.

The program first reads the contents of the TYPES.PRN file in order to provide a list of variables for the

```
/FI
```

command. (The TYPES.PRN file contains information about whether the data is numeric or text.) The FIELDS.PRN file provides the variables for the PRN files to import.

Moving files from 1-2-3 to dBASE III is not much more than the same procedure, but backward. The only change to the macro should be

```
/PF
```

with the usual parameters such as NAME, REPLACE (if the file already exists), RANGE, and GO. dBASE III can then access the files with the command line

```
APPEND FROM filename.PRN SDF
```

Creating Secure Systems

Very often, programmers are told that certain files are sensitive and should be made "snoop proof." Voila. We are now in the computer security business. The easiest method of securing files is to encrypt them. Fortunately, you can RUN a program for data and program security from dBASE III.

The methods of data encryption can range from the sublime to the ridiculous. You have to consider public versus private key encryption methods and decide who assigns the keys, among other things. Often, these questions become political issues; you may want to leave the decision to the customer.

Several useful programs on the market can handle this job for you. When a customer asks specifically for one encryption method, you may want to recommend some off-the-shelf software, unless security is your business. Most of the programs are impractical, however, because the programs require several K and boot from a disk. For this reason, these programs are difficult to use on dual floppy systems and inconvenient, at best, on hard disk systems.

The logic of data encryption is basic enough. Figure 11.4 shows a simple scrambler with obvious defeats. Some of the defeats are intentional; others are simply there. Ideally, this program would be coded in a language that can be compiled.

When pressed, I have compiled the following BASIC code and put it into service. I decided to write the code in BASIC because dBASE III handles these functions with the skill of a ballerina wrestling a lumberjack.

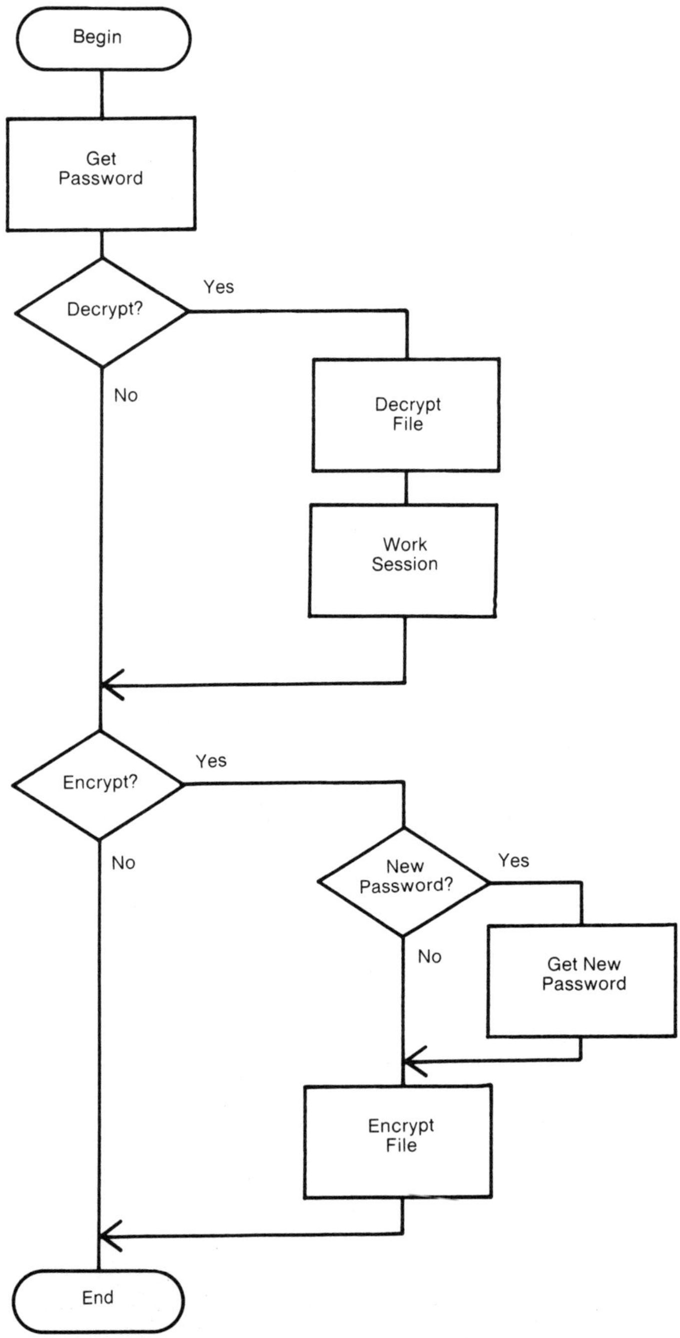

Fig. 11.4. Flowchart for a simple data-encryption system.

```
10 REM CRYPTOR.BAS
20 REM
30 P=0
40 INPUT "Your initials -> ",N$
50 INPUT "E(ncrypt) or D(ecrypt) -> ",ED$
60 INPUT "Your password (5 characters) -> ",PWORD$
70 FILE$=N$+".FLE"
80 OPEN FILE$ FOR INPUT AS 1
90 FOR X=1 TO 5
100       P=ASC(MID$(PWORD$,X,1))+P
110 NEXT
120 WHILE P>127
130      P=P-128
140 WEND
150 WHILE NOT EOF(1)
160       INPUT#1,XLATE$
170       OPEN XLATE$ FOR INPUT AS 2
180       OPEN "XLATE" FOR OUTPUT AS 3
190       WHILE NOT EOF(2)
200               IF ED$="e" OR ED$="E" THEN C=ASC(INPUT$(1,#2))+P
210               IF ED$="d" OR ED$="D" THEN C=ASC(INPUT$(1,#2))-P
220               PRINT#3,CHR$(C);
230       WEND
240       CLOSE#2
250       CLOSE#3
260       KILL XLATE$
270       NAME "XLATE" AS XLATE$
280 WEND
290 SYSTEM
```

This code is meant to be a template. I strongly advise you to modify or rewrite this code to suit your own purpose. This program was not written to deter the truly interested from accessing sensitive data; it was written to prevent the nosey from seeing what they should not.

Now to explain the code. First, initialize the encrypting variable P (line 30). Then get the user's initials. The initials plus the extension .FLE constitute a file name (lines 40, 70 through 80). The file is simply an ASCII text file containing a list of the files that a particular user can access. Next, we find out whether the files are to be encrypted or decrypted (line 50) and request the password (line 60). The program then determines an encrypting value by working some simple arithmetic with the characters in the password (lines 90 through 110). Notice that this method is nothing more than a transposition of ASCII character values. The source file is not compressed or altered in any way. Then the source file is read and translated character by character (lines 190-230). The rest of the code simply keeps things rolling until there are no more files to encrypt or decrypt.

When the BASIC program is compiled, it creates a staggering 18K file. An assembly language equivalent is listed in Appendix A.

Note: Files and data can be lost if you use an incorrect password. This danger puts a great burden on you, the programmer, to provide safe, foolproof backup capability. Lastly, remember the definition of foolproof: "Give a fool a 'foolproof' system and he'll prove you wrong."

This scrambler-descrambler program has several uses. It can descramble files either when they are first accessed or when an individual user starts work. You can also use this code to scramble and descramble PRG, NDX, FMT, and other files, although I don't usually bother unless I'm asked. Clients are usually most interested in protecting data.

CRYPTOR.BAS is RUN from dBASE III in the usual way. For the compiled version, the command is

```
RUN CRYPTOR
```

For the interpreted version, it is

```
RUN BASIC CRYPTOR
```

The second line engages the interpreter and then runs the program to be interpreted.

It is important to remember that the method described here is very elementary and is intended to serve as a guide. System and data security is best left to professionals and packaged software dedicated to that purpose.

I feel that data security, like copy-protection, is a waste of time. Both can be easily defeated when necessary. A good anecdote is the case of a software firm that openly challenged interested parties to break its encryption method. The company was even so foolish as to offer prize money to anyone capable of breaking the protection. The company went bankrupt in one month, with lots of prizes unpaid.

Epilogue

Well, how was it? Did you learn anything? Were you at least entertained?

I was repeatedly asked what this book was about while I was writing it. My standard reply was, "It's a mystery: the programmer did it, and the computer dies in the end."

I hope nothing like that happens to you, and I do hope you have benefitted from this book. And I hope you prosper when you go on your next programming gig.

A
CRYPTOR.ASM

The listing in this appendix results from running the CRYPTOR.BAS program (Chapter 11) through the IBM Personal Computer BASIC Compiler. The ASM file provides an adequate translation, so I haven't included copious notes. The following listing provides the information necessary for recoding for the 8086 assembler and for making changes to ensure code integrity.

```
Offset    Data   Source Line              IBM Personal Computer BASIC Compiler V1.00

001A      0002    10 REM ENCRYPTOR/DECRYPTOR PROGRAM
001A      0002    20 REM
001A      0002    30 P=0
0026       **              I00001:   CALL   $531
002B       **              L00010:
002B       **              L00020:
002B       **              L00030:   MOV    DI,OFFSET P!
002E       **                        MOV    SI,OFFSET <const>
0031       **                        INT    0A6H
0033      0006    40 INPUT "Your initials -> ",N$
0033       **              L00040:   MOV    BX,OFFSET <const>
0036       **                        INT    0E0H
0038       **                        DB     02H
```

```
0039   **                     INT    0E2H
003B   **                     DB     01H
003C   **                     DB     07H
003D   **                     MOV    BX,OFFSET N$
0040   **                     INT    0E3H
0042   000A  50 INPUT "E(ncrypt) or D(ecrypt) -> ",ED$
0042   **           L00050:   MOV    BX,OFFSET <const>
0045   **                     INT    0E0H
0047   **                     DB     02H
0048   **                     INT    0E2H
004A   **                     DB     01H
004B   **                     DB     07H
004C   **                     MOV    BX,OFFSET ED$
004F   **                     INT    0E3H
0051   000E  60 INPUT "Your password (5 characters) -> ",PWORD$
0051   **           L00060:   MOV    BX,OFFSET <const>
0054   **                     INT    0E0H
0056   **                     DB     02H
0057   **                     INT    0E2H
0059   **                     DB     01H
005A   **                     DB     07H
005B   **                     MOV    BX,OFFSET PWORD$
005E   **                     INT    0E3H
0060   0012  70 FILE$=N$+".FLE"
0060   **           L00070:   MOV    BX,OFFSET <const>
0063   **                     MOV    AX,OFFSET N$
0066   **                     INT    80H
0068   **                     MOV    DX,OFFSET FILE$
006B   **                     INT    8CH
006D   0016  80 OPEN FILE$ FOR INPUT AS 1
006D   **           L00080:   XOR    BX,BX
006F   **                     INT    3EH
0071   **                     DB     21H
0072   **                     MOV    CX,BX
0074   **                     MOV    BX,0001H
0077   **                     MOV    DX,OFFSET FILE$
007A   **                     INT    3EH
007C   **                     DB     1FH
007D   0016  90 FOR X=1 TO 5
007D   **           L00090:   MOV    SI,OFFSET <const>
0080   **                     INT    9AH
0082   **                     JMP    I00002
0085   0016  100      P=ASC(MID$(PWORD$,X,1))+P
```

```
0085    **            I00003:
0085    **            L00100:   MOV    SI,OFFSET X!
0088    **                      INT    0A0H
008A    **                      MOV    DX,BX
008C    **                      MOV    BX,OFFSET PWORD$
008F    **                      MOV    CX,0001H
0092    **                      INT    3DH
0094    **                      DB     0AH
0095    **                      INT    0E5H
0097    **                      INT    82H
0099    **                      MOV    DI,OFFSET P!
009C    **                      INT    0ACH
009E    **                      INT    0A8H
00A0    001A   110 NEXT
00A0    **            L00110:   MOV    DI,OFFSET <const>
00A3    **                      MOV    SI,OFFSET X!
00A6    **                      INT    0AAH
00A8    **            I00002:   MOV    DI,OFFSET X!
00AB    **                      INT    0A8H
00AD    **                      MOV    SI,DI
00AF    **                      MOV    DI,OFFSET <const>
00B2    **                      INT    0CAH
00B4    **                      JNA    $-31H
00B6    001A   120 WHILE P>127
00B6    **            L00120:
00B6    **            I00004:   MOV    DI,OFFSET <const>
00B9    **                      MOV    SI,OFFSET P!
00BC    **                      INT    0CAH
00BE    **                      JA     $+03H
00C0    **                      JMP    I00005
00C3    001A   130      P=P-128
00C3    **            L00130:   MOV    DI,OFFSET <const>
00C6    **                      MOV    SI,OFFSET P!
00C9    **                      INT    0AAH
00CB    **                      MOV    DI,SI
00CD    **                      INT    0A8H
00CF    001A   140 WEND
00CF    **            L00140:   JMP    I00004
00D2    001A   150 WHILE NOT EOF(1)
00D2    **            I00005:
00D2    **            L00150:
00D2    **            I00006:   MOV    BX,0001H
00D5    **                      INT    3DH
```

```
00D7      **                       DB      2BH
00D8      **                       NOT     BX
00DA      **                       AND     BX,BX
00DC      **                       JNE     $+03H
00DE      **                       JMP     I00007
00E1    001A    160     INPUT#1,XLATE$
00E1      **            L00160:    MOV     BX,0001H
00E4      **                       INT     0E1H
00E6      **                       INT     0E2H
00E8      **                       DB      01H
00E9      **                       DB      07H
00EA      **                       MOV     BX,OFFSET XLATE$
00ED      **                       INT     0E3H
00EF    001E    170     OPEN XLATE$ FOR INPUT AS 2
00EF      **            L00170:    XOR     BX,BX
00F1      **                       INT     3EH
00F3      **                       DB      21H
00F4      **                       MOV     CX,BX
00F6      **                       MOV     BX,0002H
00F9      **                       MOV     DX,OFFSET XLATE$
00FC      **                       INT     3EH
00FE      **                       DB      1FH
00FF    001E    180     OPEN "XLATE" FOR OUTPUT AS 3
00FF      **            L00180:    MOV     BX,0001H
0102      **                       INT     3EH
0104      **                       DB      21H
0105      **                       MOV     BX,0003H
0108      **                       MOV     DX,OFFSET <const>
010B      **                       XOR     CX,CX
010D      **                       INT     3EH
010F      **                       DB      1FH
0110    001E    190     WHILE NOT EOF(2)
0110      **            L00190:
0110      **            I00008:    MOV     BX,0002H
0113      **                       INT     3DH
0115      **                       DB      2BH
0116      **                       NOT     BX
0118      **                       AND     BX,BX
011A      **                       JNE     $+03H
011C      **                       JMP     I00009
011F    001E    200            IF ED$="e" OR ED$="E" THEN
                                  C=ASC(INPUT$(1,#2))+
                P
```

```
011F    **          L00200   MOV   BX,OFFSET <const>
0122    **                   MOV   AX,OFFSET ED$
0125    **                   INT   8DH
0127    **                   MOV   DX,0000H
012A    **                   JNE   $+01H
012C    **                   DEC   DX
012D    **                   MOV   BX,OFFSET <const>
0130    **                   INT   8DH
0132    **                   MOV   CX,0000H
0135    **                   JNE   $+01H
0137    **                   DEC   CX
0138    **                   OR    CX,DX
013A    **                   AND   CX,CX
013C    **                   JNE   $+03H
013E    **                   JMP   I00010
0141    **                   MOV   BX,0001H
0144    **                   MOV   DX,0002H
0147    **                   INT   3DH
0149    **                   DB    07H
014A    **                   INT   0E5H
014C    **                   INT   82H
014E    **                   MOV   DI,OFFSET P!
0151    **                   INT   0ACH
0153    **                   MOV   DI,OFFSET C!
0156    **                   INT   0A8H
0158    0022   210       IF ED$="d" OR ED$="D"
                          THEN C=ASC(INPUT$(1,#2))-P
0158    **          I00010:
0158    **          L00210:  MOV   BX,OFFSET <const>
015B    **                   MOV   AX,OFFSET ED$
015E    **                   INT   8DH
0160    **                   MOV   DX,0000H
0163    **                   JNE   $+01H
0165    **                   DEC   DX
0166    **                   MOV   BX,OFFSET <const>
0169    **                   INT   8DH
016B    **                   MOV   CX,0000H
016E    **                   JNE   $+01H
0170    **                   DEC   CX
0171    **                   OR    CX,DX
0173    **                   AND   CX,CX
0175    **                   JNE   $+03H
0177    **                   JMP   I00011
```

```
017A    **                        MOV   BX,0001H
017D    **                        MOV   DX,0002H
0180    **                        INT   3DH
0182    **                        DB    07H
0183    **                        INT   0E5H
0185    **                        INT   82H
0187    **                        MOV   DI,OFFSET P!
018A    **                        INT   0C4H
018C    **                        MOV   DI,OFFSET C!
018F    **                        INT   0A8H
0191    0022   220          PRINT#3,CHR$(C);
0191    **              I00011:
0191    **              L00220:   MOV   BX,0003H
0194    **                        INT   0E8H
0196    **                        MOV   SI,OFFSET C!
0199    **                        INT   0A0H
019B    **                        INT   3DH
019D    **                        DB    05H
019E    **                        INT   95H
01A0    0022   230      WEND
01A0    **              L00230:   JMP   I00008
01A3    0022   240      CLOSE#2
01A3    **     I00009:
01A3    **              L00240:   MOV   BX,0002H
01A6    **                        INT   3EH
01A8    **                        DB    22H
01A9    0022   250      CLOSE#3
01A9    **              L00250:   MOV   BX,0003H
01AC    **                        INT   3EH
01AE    **                        DB    22H
01AF    0022   260      KILL XLATE$
01AF    **              L00260:   MOV   BX,OFFSET XLATE$
01B2    **                        INT   3EH
01B4    **                        DB    25H
01B5    0022   270      NAME "XLATE" AS XLATE$
01B5    **              L00270:   MOV   BX,OFFSET <const>
01B8    **                        MOV   DX,OFFSET XLATE$
01BB    **                        INT   3EH
01BD    **                        DB    24H
01BE    0022   280 WEND
01BE    **              L00280:   JMP   I00006
01C1    0022   290 SYSTEM
01C1    **              I00007:
```

```
01C1    **      L00290: INT   3EH
01C3    **              DB    01H
01C4    0022
01C4    **              INT   3EH
01C6    **              DB    02H
01C7    0022
```

B
Glossary

Application: A logical idea for which a program is designed. Each block in a flowchart is an application.

Background programming: Code that, although unseen by the user, performs about 90 percent of the actual database manipulations. The user may only see the data input and interrogation screens (the foreground programming), which are actually a small part of the overall working code.

Database: A set of information with a common link among individual members of the set.

Environment: The physical setting in which a database system is to be used.

Flowchart: A graphic representation of a program's logic.

Foreground programming: The part of the working code with which the user interacts; includes input and interrogation screens, menu systems, etc.

Indexkey: The value to be searched for in an INDEXed database.

Job: The object of a program, or the function performed by a task or group of tasks.

Keyfield: The database field that is INDEXed ON.

Masterbase: A large database that contains detailed information on each member of a group of databases. A database fits a unique need, but a masterbase is a storage tank for several databases.

Menu system: A set of linked foreground tasks that provides the user with some control over the database system.

Module: The code that is generated to perform a task.

Primary key: The KEYFIELD the computer uses to keep track of a record. dBASE III uses RECNO( ) as a primary key.

Qualifier: A restrictor in a command line that directs the command to perform its operation on a subset of the whole database. When you use these words with a condition, they qualify the information to be processed:

```
REPLACE ALL LASTNAME WITH "Kramden" FOR FIRSTNAME="Ralph"
```

Random access : A method of organizing a database wherein the user controls the order and organization of records.

Secondary key: The KEYFIELD humans use to keep track of records. Usually our KEYFIELDs are randomly oriented: We keep track of things by name (or address, value, etc.), not by the position in a database.

Sequential access: The computer's method of organizing and ordering a database. The computer and dBASE III use a FIFO (first in, first out) ordering system.

Subroutine: A program specifically designed or modified for one application or environment.

Task: A general program that can be easily adapted as a subroutine or a job.

Working code: The final, debugged version of a program.

C
A Database Access Template

```
***MAIN.PRG CALLED FROM WRITE.PRG
SET PROC TO VIADEDPA
**
DO WHILE .T.
CLEAR
TEXT
 ==================================================================
 ||                MAIN  MENU                                    ||
 ==================================================================
 ||                                                              ||
 ||                      Ø. Exit                                 ||
 ||                      1. View                                 ||
 ||                      2. Add                                  ||
 ||                      3. Edit                                 ||
 ||                      4. Pack                                 ||
 ||                                                              ||
 ||                                                              ||
 ==================================================================
```

```
ENDTEXT
**
DO CASE
CASE "&database"="MAGAZINE"
@ 10,32 SAY "5. Print Magazines by Audience"
selectnum=6
**
CASE "&database"="BOOKS"
@ 10,32 SAY "5. Print Publishers by Audience"
selectnum=6
**
CASE "&database"="SENDWHER"
@ 10,32 SAY "5. Match Manuscripts to Markets"
selectnum=6
**
OTHE
selectnum=5
ENDC
number=selectnum-1
**
DO WHILE selectnum < 0 .OR. selectnum > number
select=" "
@ 12,33 SAY " select : : "
@ 12,42 GET select PICTURE "#"
READ
selectnum=VAL(select)
ENDD
**
DO CASE
**
CASE selectnum= 0
CLEA ALL
RETU
**
CASE selectnum= 1
USE &database INDEX &INDEX
CLEAR
@ 1, 0 SAY "V I E W"
@ 1,60 SAY "TODAY IS ->"
@ 1,72 SAY DTOC(DATE())
DO &FRAMER
IF (EOF() .OR. BOF())
select=" "
```

```
@ 21,0 SAY "EMPTY DATA FILE"
@ 22,0 SAY "Strike any key to continue..." ;
GET select
READ
ELSE
DO &GETTER
CLEA GETS
poschoice="X"
**
DO WHILE poschoice <> " "
DO POSITION
ENDD
ENDI
USE
**
CASE selectnum= 2
**
DO CASE
CASE "&database"="MAGAZINE"
USE MAGAZINE INDEX MAGAZINE, AUDIENCE
**
CASE "&database"="BOOKS"
USE BOOKS INDEX BOOKS, BOOKAUDS
**
OTHER
USE &database INDEX &INDEX
ENDC
adder="&database"+. "add"
COPY STRUCTURE TO ADDER
SELE B
USE ADDER
CLEAR
@ 1, 0 SAY "A D D"
@ 1,60 SAY "Today is ->"
@ 1,72 SAY DTOC(DATE())
DO &FRAMER
@ 21,0 SAY "Press <control-W> to exit"
addchoice="X"
**
DO WHILE addchoice <> " "
APPEND BLANK
DO &GETTER
READ
```

```
addchoice=TRIM(&indexkey)
ENDD
DELETE
USE
SELE A
APPEND FROM ADDER
USE
**
CASE selectnum= 3
USE &database INDEX &INDEX
CLEAR
@ 1, 0 SAY "E D I T"
@ 1,60 SAY "Today is ->"
@ 1,72 SAY DTOC(DATE())
DO &FRAMER
IF (EOF() .OR. BOF())
select=" "
@ 21,0 SAY "Empty Data File"
@ 22,0 SAY "Strike any key to continue..." ;
GET select
READ
ELSE
DO &GETTER
CLEA GETS
DO EDITOR
ENDI
USE
**
CASE selectnum= 4
DO PACKER
**
CASE selectnum= 5
**
DO CASE
CASE "&database"="MAGAZINE"
SET CONSOLE OFF
USE MAGAZINE INDEX AUDIENCE
REPORT FORM MAGAUDS NOEJECT TO PRINT
SET CONSOLE ON
**
CASE "&database"="BOOKS"
SET CONSOLE OFF
USE BOOKS INDEX BOOKAUDS
```

```
148: REPORT FORM BOOKAUDS NOEJECT TO PRINT
149: SET CONSOLE ON
150: **
151: CASE "&database"="SENDWHER"
152: DO SENDWHER
153: ENDC
154: ENDC
155: ENDD
```

Line 2 SETs the PROCEDURE file to VIADEDPA, which is an acronym for VIew, ADd, EDit, PAck. I'm not requesting any information from the user, so my menu is created with TEXT . . . ENDTEXT. This routine accesses a database, so the only options are those listed.

If special databases are passed to the program, however, some extra options must be made available. For this reason, I included the DO CASE code in lines 21 through 36. I always pass the names of variables from the main program, so my USE and INDEX commands are no more than MACRO substitutions.

Lines 59, 97, and 119 call the subroutine, FRAMER, which is also declared in the calling program. FRAMER is simply a method of creating a workable screen. Similarly, the GETTER subroutine listed on lines 67, 103, and 127 GETs information from database to user and vice versa.

I always pack a lot of work into a little code. An example of that is in lines 81 and 84, where I activate two indexfiles for each database I open. The first indexfile is the one necessary for the job at hand. The second indexfile is there to make sure the first is updated when the job is done.

dBASE III can't place new data in an existing database and make it appear when the KEYFIELDS dictate, so I COPY the STUCTURE of my database to a tank and APPEND from there, as shown in lines 89 to 111.

When I'm generating a report (lines 142 and 148), I don't need the CONSOLE on, so I turn it OFF in lines 140 and 146. I'm usually very careful about the data that goes into and out of my printer, so I use NOEJECT in lines 142 and 149. Similarly, because I am so careful about my printer, I EJECT after I'm through REPORTing in lines 143 and 150.

D

A Label- and Envelope-Maker Template

```
**LABEL/ENVELOPE GENERATOR, LABEL2.PRG
PON=.F.
CLEA
ACCEPT "Output to S(creen), P(rinter) or Q(uit)? -> " to select
**
DO CASE
CASE UPPER(select) = "S"
**
CASE UPPER(select) = "P"
PON=.T.
OTHE
RETU
ENDC
ACCEPT "Output to L(abels) or E(nvelopes)? -> " to select
**
DO WHILE .T.
condition=" "
**
```

```
DO WHILE condition = " "
CLEA
@ 2, 0 SAY "A D D R E S S   G E N E R A T O R"
@ 2,72 SAY DTOC(DATE())
@ 3, 0 SAY "========================================"
@ 3,40 SAY "========================================"
DO BMFRAMES
DO BMGETS
CLEA GETS
@ 19,0 SAY 'EXAMPLE :STATE="CA", <RETURN> = ALL ENTRIES, "QUIT" = QUIT'
@ 21,0
@ 20,0 SAY "-"
ACCEPT "Enter condition " TO condition
@ 19,0
condition=TRIM(condition)
**
DO CASE
CASE UPPER(condition) = "QUIT"
RETU
**
CASE TYPE("&condition")="U"
CLEA GETS
@ 22,0
select=" "
@ 22,0 SAY "Invalid Expression: "+ ;
"Press <RETURN> to continue..." ;
GET select
READ
@ 22,0
conditon= " "
ENDC
ENDD
LOCATE ALL FOR &condition
**
IF PON
SET PRINT ON
SET CONSOLE OFF
ELSE
CLEA
ENDI
**
DO CASE
CASE UPPER(SELECT)='L'
```

```
**
DO WHILE .NOT. EOF()
extra=0
**
IF TRIM(CONTACT) <> " "
? TRIM(CONTACT)+', '+TRIM(POSITION)
ELSE
? POSITION
ENDI
? NAME
? ADDRESS1
**
IF TRIM(ADDRESS2) <> " "
? ADDRESS2
ELSE
extra=extra+1
ENDI
? TRIM(CITY)+', '+STATE+'   '+ZIPCODE
**
IF TRIM(COUNTRY) <> " "
? COUNTRY
ELSE
extra=extra+1
ENDI
**
DO WHILE extra > 0
?
extra=extra-1
ENDD
CONTINUE
ENDD
**
CASE UPPER(SELECT)='E'
gap=SPACE(30)
**
DO WHILE .NOT. EOF()
extra=2
?
?
?
?
?
? 'Joseph-David Carrabis'
```

```
105: ? 'JDI, INC.'
106: ? 'PO Box 396'
107: ? 'Hanover, NH 03755'
108: ?
109: ?
110: ?
111: ?
112: **
113: IF TRIM(CONTACT) <> " "
114: ? GAP+ TRIM(CONTACT)+', '+TRIM(POSITION)
115: ELSE
116: ? GAP+ POSITION
117: ENDI
118: ? GAP+ NAME
119: ? GAP+ ADDRESS1
120: **
121: IF TRIM(ADDRESS2) <> " "
122: ? GAP+ ADDRESS2
123: ELSE
124: extra=extra+1
125: ENDI
126: ? GAP+ TRIM(CITY)+', '+STATE+'    '+ZIPCODE
127: **
128: IF TRIM(COUNTRY) <> " "
129: ? GAP+ COUNTRY
130: ELSE
131: extra=extra+1
132: ENDI
133: **
134: DO WHILE extra > 0
135: ?
136: extra=extra-1
137: ENDD
138: CONTINUE
139: ENDD
140: ENDC
141: PON=.F.
142: SET PRINT OFF
143: SET CONSOLE ON
144: ENDD
```

When starting the program, I don't know whether I will need the printer, so I create a logical variable in line 2 to determine whether the printer should be on. Sending output to the screen requires no special treatment, so none is given in lines 7 and 8.

Line 39 is interesting: I check errors by finding out whether a requested condition exists by determining the TYPE( ) of the condition. An undefined condition TYPE( ) qualifies as an error condition.

After that, the program merely prints out one-up labels or envelopes. You could modify this routine for three-up, five-up, and so on. That bit of code can be easily modified with MACROs:

```
STORE name TO ALLNAME
STORE address1 TO ALLONE
STORE address2 TO ALLTWO
STORE TRIM(city)+", "+state+"  "+zipcode to ALLELSE
SKIP
```

Are you getting the idea? We're creating macros with ALLNAME, ALLONE, ALLTWO, and ALLELSE. The rest of the program becomes:

```
STORE ALLNAME+name TO ALLNAME
STORE ALLONE+address1 TO ALLONE
STORE ALLTWO+address2 TO ALLTWO
STORE ALLELSE+TRIM(city)+"' "+state+"  "+zipcode TO ALLELSE
SKIP
STORE ALLNAME+name TO ALLNAME
STORE ALLONE+address1 TO ALLONE
STORE ALLTWO+address2 TO ALLTWO
STORE ALLELSE+TRIM(city)+"' "+state+"  "+zipcode TO ALLELSE
? ALLNAME
? ALLONE
? ALLTWO
? ALLELSE
??
```

You can enhance this method by predetermining the size of the fields or creating a GAP variable, such as was used in the previous example.

E
A Template for a WordStar MailMerge Module

```
**MLMRGE.PRG
**
DO WHILE .T.
CLEAR
ACCEPT "Which database do you want to use?" TO database
STOR TRIM(UPPER(database)) TO database
IF database="QUIT"
RETU
ENDI
USE &database
@ 11,0 SAY ' '
ACCEPT "What subset do you want?" to subset
STOR TRIM(subset) TO subset
**
**
```

```
16: DO CASE
17: CASE AT(subset,'QUIT quit')=0
18: RETU
19: **
20: CASE TYPE(&subset)="U"
21: **
22: DO WHILE TYPE(&subset)="U"
23: @ 12,0
24: @ 12,0 SAY "INVALID EXPRESSION"
25: WAIT
26: @ 12,0
27: @ 11,0 SAY ' '
28: ACCEPT "What subset do you want?" to subset
29: IF UPPER("&subset")="QUIT"
30: RETU
31: ENDI
32: ENDD
33: **
34: OTHE
35: COPY TO A:MLMRGE.DAT SDF DELIMITED WITH , FIELD CONTACT, POSITION, ;
36: NAME, ADDRESS1, CITY, STATE, ZIPCODE, DEAR FOR &subset
37: COPY TO A:SAMNA.DAT SDF DELIMITED WITH / FIELD CONTACT, POSITION, ;
38: NAME,ADDRESS1, CITY, STATE, ZIPCODE FOR &subset
39: @ 14,0 SAY 'Done.'
40: WAIT
41: ENDC
42: ENDD
```

You always need to know what tools to use, so I ask that right away in line 5. Line 17 demonstrates the use of a substring search in place of a logical condition.

Again, an undefined TYPE is used in lines 20 and 22 as an error check. If no errors or stops are encountered, the main body of the program is engaged in lines 35 and 37. Here files are created for two word processors, WordStar and SAMNA. These files will be used to produce mailmerge documents.

F
A "Where Sent" Template for Tracking Manuscripts

This module matches manuscripts to markets (magazines that might buy the manuscripts) and shows an example of resource planning and tracking. The module takes available resources—the manuscripts—and finds places where those resources will prosper—magazine markets. Then the user can track the progress of those resources.

```
**SENDWHERE.PRG FOR MATCHING MANUSCRIPTS TO MARKETS
SELE A
USE MAGAZINE INDEX AUDIENCE
SELE B
USE SENDWHER INDEX MSSNAME
GOTO TOP
**
DO WHILE .NOT. EOF()
NUMBER=1
```

```
AUD=AUDIENCE
CLEAR
? MSS_NAME
SELECT A
FIND &AUD
**
DO WHILE AUDIENCE = AUD
**
IF NUMBER=21
SELE B
CARRYNAME=MSS_NAME
INSERT BLANK
REPL MORE WITH .T.
REPL MSS_NAME WITH CARRYNAME
REPL AUDIENCE WITH AUD
NUMBER=1
SELECT A
ENDI
**
IF NUMBER < 10
FIELDNAME="T"+STR(NUMBER, 1, 0)
ELSE
FIELDNAME="T"+STR(NUMBER, 2, 0)
ENDI
MAGNAME=NAME
SELE B
REPL &FIELDNAME WITH MAGNAME
? MAGNAME
NUMBER=NUMBER+1
SELECT A
SKIP
ENDD
SELE B
SKIP
ENDD
CLEA
ACCEPT "PRINT REPORT [(A)ll/(S)ingle/(N)one)? -> " TO PRINTREPT
PRINTREPT=UPPER(PRINTREPT)
**
DO CASE
CASE PRINTREPT='A'
GOTO TOP
**
```

```
53: DO WHILE .NOT. EOF()
54: DO SENDWHER.FMT
55: SKIP
56: ENDD
57: **
58: CASE PRINTREPT='S'
59: ANOTHER=.T.
60: **
61: DO WHILE ANOTHER
62: ACCEPT "What is the manuscript's name ('Q' to QUIT)? -> " TO PMSSNAME
63: PMSSNAME=UPPER(PMSSNAME)
64: **
65: IF PMSSNAME = 'Q'
66: RETU
67: ELSE
68: FIND &PMSSNAME
69: DO SENDWHER.FMT
70: ENDI
71: ACCEPT "Do another? ->" TO ANOTHER
72: ENDD
73: ENDC
74: RETU
```

The lines of major interest are 30 and 32, the fieldname building lines. Lines 58 to 73 permit the selective viewing or printing of format files based on manuscript name. You can use these lines as a template for selective file generation.

G
A Main Menu Template

```
***WRITE.PRG MAIN DRIVER
SET EXAC ON
SET TALK OFF
SET BELL OFF
SET DELIMITER OFF
**
DO WHILE .T.
CLEAR
TEXT
============================================================
||        W R I T E !   W R I T E !   W R I T E !        ||
============================================================
||                     0. Quit to System                  ||
||                     1. Quit to dBASE                   ||
||                     2. Quit to WordStar                ||
||                     3. Magazine Menu                   ||
||                     4. Book Publisher Menu             ||
||                     5. Get Subset for Mailmerge        ||
||                     6. Make Labels/Envelopes           ||
||                     7. Send What to Who                ||
||                                                        ||
==========================select : :=======================
```

```
ENDT
selectnum=8
**
DO WHILE selectnum < 0 .OR. selectnum >  7
select=" "
@ 14,40 GET select PICTURE "#"
READ
selectnum=VAL(select)
ENDD
**
DO CASE
CASE selectnum= 0
QUIT
**
CASE selectnum= 1
CLEA ALL
RETU
**
CASE SELECTNUM= 2
RUN WS
**
CASE selectnum= 3
STOR "MAGAZINE" TO database, index
framer="BMFRAMES"
getter="BMGETS"
keyfield=NAME"
DO MAIN
**
CASE selectnum= 4
STOR "BOOKS" TO database, index
framer="BMFRAMES"
getter="BMGETS"
keyfield=NAME"
DO MAIN
**
CASE selectnum= 5
DO MLMRGE
**
CASE selectnum= 6
CLEAR
Accept "Which database do you want to use?" TO database
USE &DATABASE
DO LABEL2
```

```
67: **
68: CASE SELECTNUM= 7
69: database="SENDWHER"
70: index="MSSNAME"
71: framer="SEFRAME"
72: getter="SEGETS"
73: keyfield="MSS_NAME"
74: DO MAIN
75: ENDC
76: ENDD
```

This is the main program from which all others are called. This program starts and stops each session for the client, so I SET many conditions at the beginning (lines 2 to 5).

We request no messages from the user, so the menu is created with TEXT . . . ENDTEXT lines (9 to 24) instead of a series of @@ SAY. . . GETs.

The DO CASE . . . ENDCASE construction that runs the length of the program (lines 27 to 76) uses the PUBLIC command without specifying it. The key is that variables become PUBLIC to all called programs. I don't want the variables to be changed, so I declare them without the use of the PUBLIC command.

H
Examples of FRAMER and GETTER Routines

A Typical FRAMER Routine

```
*** BMFRAMES.PRG
@  4, 0 SAY "Name:"
@  5, 0 SAY "Address1:"
@  6, 0 SAY "Address2:"
@  7, 0 SAY "City:"
@  7,40 SAY "State:"
@  7,54 SAY "Zip:"
@  8, 0 SAY "Country:"
@  8,40 SAY "Phone:"
@ 10, 0 SAY "Contact:"
@ 10,50 SAY "Dear:"
@ 11, 0 SAY "Position:"
@ 12, 0 SAY "Audience:"
@ 12,40 SAY "Mss Length:"
@ 14, 0 SAY "Qry:"
```

```
@ 14,10 SAY "Mss:"
@ 14,20 SAY "SmS:"
@ 14,30 SAY "DMP:"
@ 14,40 SAY "Gdl:"
@ 14,52 SAY "Source:"
@ 16, 0 SAY "Comment:"
RETURN
```

A Typical GETTER Routine

```
*** BMGETS.PRG
IF DELETE()
@ 1,30 SAY "DELETED"
ELSE
@ 1,30 SAY "       "
ENDIF
*
@  4, 7 GET name
@  5,10 GET address1
@  6,10 GET address2
@  7, 6 GET city
@  7,47 GET state
@  7,59 GET zipcode
@  8, 9 GET Country
@  8,47 GET phone
@ 10, 9 GET contact
@ 10,55 GET dear
@ 11,10 GET position
@ 12,10 GET audience
@ 12,52 GET msslength
@ 14, 5 GET gry
@ 14,15 GET mss
@ 14,25 GET sms
@ 14,35 GET dmp
@ 14,45 GET gdl
@ 14,60 GET source
@ 16, 9 GET comment
RETURN
```

I
MAGAZINE.DBF and SENDWHER.DBF for Appendixes D through H

```
Structure for database : A:MAGAZINE.DBF
Number of data records :       Ø
Date of last update    : ØØ/ØØ/ØØ
Field  Field name  Type        Width    Dec
1  NAME          Character     5Ø
2  ADDRESS1      Character     5Ø
3  ADDRESS2      Character     5Ø
4  CITY          Character     3Ø
5  STATE         Character      2
6  COUNTRY       Character     2Ø
7  ZIPCODE       Character     1Ø
8  CONTACT       Character     3Ø
9  DEAR          Character     2Ø
1Ø  AUDIENCE      Character     3Ø
11  PHONE         Character     15
12  GDL           Character      1
13  POSITION      Character     2Ø
14  QRY           Character      1
```

```
15  MSS          Character      1
16  SMS          Character      1
17  DMP          Character      1
18  MSSLENGTH    Character     20
19  SOURCE       Character     20
20  COMMENT      Character    151
** Total **                     524

Structure for database : A:SENDWHER.DBF
Number of data records :        0
Date of last update    : 00/00/00
Field  Field name  Type       Width    Dec
1  MSS_NAME     Character     30
2  AUDIENCE     Character     30
3  MORE         Logical        1
4  T1           Character     30
5  T2           Character     30
6  T3           Character     30
7  T4           Character     30
8  T5           Character     30
9  T6           Character     30
10  T7           Character     30
11  T8           Character     30
12  T9           Character     30
13  T10          Character     30
14  T11          Character     30
15  T12          Character     30
16  T13          Character     30
Press any key to continue...
17  T14          Character     30
18  T15          Character     30
19  T16          Character     30
20  T17          Character     30
21  T18          Character     30
22  T19          Character     30
23  T20          Character     30
24  M            Numeric       10
25  C1           Character     75
26  C2           Character     75
27  C3           Character     75
28  C4           Character     75
** Total **                     972
```

J
Function Keys and Their Equivalent ASCII Values

Key	*ASCII Value*
F2	254
F3	253
F4	252
F5	251
F6	250
F7	249
F8	248
F9	247
F10	246

You can also intercept F1 with the WAIT TO variable name command. The value returned is zero. Because other keys might also return a zero to WAIT, you must ensure that any other keys returning zero are trapped.

K
The SED Utility

SED, the Screen EDitor shipped with updates of dBASE III, takes dBASE commands you insert in the screen display and converts them into a workable dBASE III program. The commands are inserted by enclosing them in brackets ([ ]). The programming therefore is still up to you, to some extent. SED's function, then, is that of a screen and form generator. You enter what you want where you want it, much as you do with the ZIP utility of dBASE II. SED then converts your display into a dBASE III program you can DO.

Before SED can be run, it has to be installed using the SINSTALL.EXE program. The procedure is not complicated; SINSTALL does most of the work for you. Those with a serious interest in modifying programs so that they do special things will have ample opportunity with SINSTALL. Note that SED can create both PRG and CMD files. During installation, you are prompted to indicate which default SED should use. Be careful when declaring the kind of monitor you use; SED treats a 16-intensity green monitor as a full-color monitor.

Provided you have a minimum of 320K of memory, you can start SED from inside dBASE III by typing RUN SED. You can also start it from DOS by simply typing SED at the DOS prompt.

SED has a variety of commands, most of which can be found on page 60 of the on-line manual. Page 66 of the manual summarizes the commands. This page can also be accessed from within SED by typing Alt-H (the SED HELP command). But SED suffers from a major problem: the directory lists pages that are not accessible. Page 90 is listed, for instance, but no page 90 exists. Trying to get to page 90 will produce a frustrating error message.

Once you've experimented with the commands, you have no real need to wade through the entire 200 screen pages (96 main pages, each with about 3 screens).

The commands serve two purposes: moving the cursor and drawing boxes and lines. The cursor-movement commands follow their own logic, which differs from the logic used in dBASE II or III. The only similarity between dBASE's cursor movement and SED's cursor movement is that both use the WordStar "magic diamond" (Ctrl-E, Ctrl-X, Ctrl-S, Ctrl-D).

The best feature of SED is that you can draw nice boxes, squares, lines, and so on. First get SED running. Then enter *N* (for New file) and *TEST*. SED will drop you into a screen that is blank except for a prompt line at the top and a blinking cursor. I happen to feel that the prompt line is worthless without the addition of cursor location information. The line-and-column position of the cursor is displayed when you enter Alt-P.

Now you can begin to draw your boxes and lines. Both boxes and lines are generated through the use of two keystroke combinations. In both cases, the first keystroke is ^B (Ctrl-B). You start a box or line with ^BB (BLOCK BEGIN) and end it with ^BE (BLOCK END). Make sure that the BLOCK END marker is placed properly with regard to the BLOCK BEGIN marker. For a line, BLOCK END must be to the right of BLOCK BEGIN; for a box, BLOCK END must be below BLOCK END and to the right of it. Otherwise, you'll get an error message.

The next keystroke combination is ^BF (BLOCK FILL). You'll be asked what character to use to draw the line or fill the block. Here SED demonstrates an interesting feature: you can draw lines or fill boxes with control codes.

How is this capability useful? For example, you can use ^G (the bell) to send an error message without altering the screen. You can also place printer control codes in the file, as well as printer and screen graphics codes. Those codes can produce some attractive displays. A little experimenting shows that there are happy faces, sad faces, diamonds, stars, arrows, and other interesting characters masquerading as control codes. Do remember, however, that the code that prints a happy face on the screen may cause your printer to throw twenty pages.

The following code was input to SED:

```
[SET TALK OFF][CLEAR][USE CUSTOMER][COPY STRUC TO TEMP][USE TEMP][**]
[NEWNAME='X' ][DO WHILE LEN(TRIM(NEWNAME))<>0][APPEND BLANK]
CUSTOMER INFORMATION
---------------------------------------------------------------------------
---Name        <name
Address <address
City        <city                                State <state ZIP<zipcode

Home phone <hphone
Busi phone <bphone

Active <active

Other  <other

---------------------------------------------------------------------------
[READ][NEWNAME=NAME][ENDD][DELE][USE CUSTOMER][APPE FROM TEMP][ERAS TEMP.DBF]
```

And here is the resulting program:

```
* DB3TEST.PRG
SET TALK OFF
CLEAR
USE CUSTOMER
COPY STRUC TO TEMP
USE TEMP
**
NEWNAME='X'
DO WHILE LEN(TRIM(NEWNAME))<>0
```

```
APPEND BLANK
@ 1,1 SAY "CUSTOMER INFORMATION"
@ 2,1 SAY "------------------------------------------------------"
@ 2,56 SAY "-----------------------"
@ 3,1 SAY "Name"
@ 3,10 GET name
@ 4,1 SAY "Address"
@ 4,10 GET address
@ 5,1 SAY "City"
@ 5,10 GET city
@ 5,42 SAY "State"
@ 5,49 GET state
@ 5,55 SAY "Zip"
@ 5,59 GET zipcode
@ 7,1 SAY "Home phone"
@ 7,13 GET hphone
@ 8,1 SAY "Busi phone"
@ 8,13 GET bphone
@ 10,1 SAY "Active"
@ 10,9 GET active
@ 12,1 SAY "Other"
@ 12,9 GET other
@ 14,1 SAY "------------------------------------------------------"
@ 14,56 SAY "-----------------------"
READ
NEWNAME=NAME
ENDD
DELE
USE CUSTOMER
APPE FROM TEMP
ERAS TEMP.DBF
```

Despite its cumbersome command structures, SED is a useful tool. Blocks and lines can be copied, erased, and moved without difficulty. With SED, custom format files are easy to create; those capabilities make learning SED worthwhile.

Index

MORE COMPUTER KNOWLEDGE FROM QUE

IBM PC Expansion & Software Guide

"This may well be the most comprehensive software directory of its kind. The *IBM PC Expansion & Software Guide* is a directory to be trusted."

PC Magazine/March 19, 1985

Containing descriptions of 7,666 products for the IBM and PC compatibles, Que Corporation's expanded guide, now in its 6th edition, has grown with each publication. It provides major listings for hardware, software products, supplies and services, and IBM PC dealers. Company and product questionnaires give readers the opportunity to contribute information and ask questions.

C Programming Guide, 2nd Edition

by Jack Purdum

Keep up-to-date on the latest developments in the C programming language with this revised edition of the best-selling *C Programming Guide*. This popular tutorial shows you the secrets of experts—the tips, tricks, and techniques that take so long to learn on your own. Gain the knowledge and skill you need to venture into all areas of programming, from operating systems to accounting packages.

PC DOS User's Guide

by Chris DeVoney

Become more skilled in using your IBM PC and its most basic software program, the Disk Operating System. This best-selling guide covers both the simple and advanced features of PC DOS, Version 2.0. The book's concise explanations will help you master each of the PC DOS commands and understand such topics as the PC DOS hierarchical directory and I/O redirection. This clearly written and easy-to-use book has proved to be a valuable asset for many PC users.

Networking IBM PCs: A Practical Guide

by Michael Durr

Networking IBM PCs is a superb guide to the important features of local area networking. From this book you can learn how to select, install, use, and manage a local area network for IBM PCs and PC compatibles. Critical management issues, including risks and benefits, security, hardware organization, mainframe accessing, and much more, are discussed. If you have not yet invested in a networking system, this book will help you evaluate before buying.

Item	Title	Price	Quantity	Extension
189	IBM PC Expansion & Software Guide, 6th Edition	$21.95		
188	C Programming Guide, 2nd Edition	$19.95		
30	PC DOS User's Guide	$16.95		
125	Networking IBM PCs: A Practical Guide	$18.95		
			Book Subtotal	
			Shipping & Handling ($1.75 per item)	
			Indiana Residents Add 5% Sales Tax	
			GRAND TOTAL	

Method of Payment:

☐ Check ☐ VISA ☐ MasterCard ☐ American Express

Card Number ____________________ Exp. Date ____________________

Cardholder Name ____

Ship to ____

Address ____

City ____________________ State ____________ ZIP ____________

If you can't wait, call **1-800-428-5331** and order TODAY.

All prices subject to change without notice.

DBAP-8510

FOLD HERE

Place
Stamp
Here

Que Publishing, Inc.
7999 Knue Road
Indianapolis, IN 46250

NEW TECHNIQUES FOR PROFESSIONALS

IBM PC UPDATE

INNOVATIVE . . . INFORMATIVE . . . USEFUL

That's what today's professionals are saying about *IBM PC UPDATE*.

And well they should. No other monthly periodical offers PC users as much quality information as *UPDATE* packs into every issue. Designed for today's professionals, *UPDATE* is a dynamic, valuable resource.

INNOVATIVE . . . and unique, *UPDATE*'s segmented approach provides convenience. Each clearly defined section is easy to find and offers practical information on one of *UPDATE*'s featured topics: word processing, spreadsheets, data base management, and integrated software.

INFORMATIVE . . . articles keep you up-to-date on the latest hardware and software releases and provide useful information on important existing products.

USEFUL . . . skill-building information helps you improve productivity and increase your proficiency on the PC. Monthly columns give you expert advice for maximizing the potential of applications programs such as dBASE, WordStar, 1-2-3, Symphony, and Framework.

Read *IBM PC UPDATE*. This is one publication today's professional can't afford to miss.

SUBSCRIBE TODAY

ORDER FORM

IBM PC UPDATE
New Techniques for Professionals

	Price	Qty.	Extension
12 issues (inside the United States)	$48.00		
24 issues (inside the United States)	$72.00		
12 issues (outside the United States)	$68.00		
24 issues (outside the United States)	$92.00		

que

Que Publishing, Inc.
7999 Knue Road
Indianapolis, IN 46250
317/842-7162
800/227-7999

TOTAL ______

Method of Payment:

Check ☐ VISA ☐ MasterCard ☐ AMEX ☐ Bill me ☐

Card Number ______________ Exp. Date ______________

Cardholder Name ______________

Ship to ______________

Address ______________

City ______________ State ______________ ZIP ______________

All prices subject to change without notice.

DBAP-8510